PSYCHOLOGICAL TESTS
AND
SOCIAL WORK PRACTICE

PSYCHOLOGICAL TESTS
AND
SOCIAL WORK PRACTICE

An Introductory Guide

By

MORTON L. ARKAVA, Ph.D.

Chairman and Professor
Department of Social Work
University of Montana
Missoula, Montana

and

MARK SNOW, Ph.D.

Professor
Department of Psychology
Boise State University
Boise, Idaho

CHARLES C THOMAS • PUBLISHER
Springfield • Illinois • U.S.A.

Published and Distributed Throughout the World by
CHARLES C THOMAS ● PUBLISHER
Bannerstone House
301-327 East Lawrence Avenue, Springfield, Illinois, U.S.A.

© *1978, by* CHARLES C THOMAS ● PUBLISHER
ISBN 0-398-03832-5 (cloth)
ISBN 0-398-03839-2 (paper)
Library of Congress Catalog Card Number: 78-16924

With THOMAS BOOKS *careful attention is given to all details of manufacturing and design. It is the Publisher's desire to present books that are satisfactory as to their physical qualities and artistic possibilities and appropriate for their particular use.* THOMAS BOOKS *will be true to those laws of quality that assure a good name and good will.*

Printed in the United States of America
V-R-1

Library of Congress Cataloging in Publication Data

Arkava, Morton L
    Psychological tests and social work practice.

    Includes index.
    1. Psychological tests. 2. Social service.
I. Snow, Mark, joint author. II. Title.
BF176.A74   152.8   78-16924
ISBN 0-398-03832-5
ISBN 0-398-03839-2 pbk.

PREFACE

THE production and utilization of educational and psychological tests have increased dramatically since their development more than seventy years ago. Greater numbers of tests are being used to evaluate and guide individuals and aid in administrative decisions. Workers in the social services today will confront the results of various kinds of psychological and educational tests, since most case histories in use contain test information.

Because many persons currently practicing in the social services lack basic educational preparation in test use, they tend to misuse and underutilize test information. It is imperative that persons engaged in the delivery of human services understand some simple test concepts for use in effective case management.

This introductory guide was developed to help the social service practitioner use test results more rationally and consistently. It is not intended to serve as a comprehensive textbook on psychological test administration, interpretation, or utilization, but rather to serve as a basic guide for those persons who have little or no background in the use and interpretation of psychological and educational tests. For those who have had graduate-level coursework in psychological testing or extensive in-service training, advanced texts on the subject are advised.

The authors acknowledge the contributions of Ms. Genie Brier. We are grateful for her editorial guidance and many suggestions.

CONTENTS

PSYCHOLOGICAL TESTS
AND
SOCIAL WORK PRACTICE

CHAPTER 1

PURPOSES OF TESTING

WHAT IS A TEST?

CRONBACH, a noted authority on testing, has defined a test as "a systematic procedure for comparing the behavior of two or more individuals."* Others have defined tests as standardized procedures for obtaining a sample of an individual's behavior. Psychologists and others use tests in order to predict what a person might do or to discover what he could do (predictions). Similarly, tests may help reveal why a person does certain things. While undoubtedly the answers to these questions would be more accurate if the individuals involved could be observed over a long period, this generally is not practical in clinical or industrial settings. One must there-

*L. J. Cronbach. "New Light on Test Strategy from Decision Theory," *Proceedings of 1954 Invitational Conference on Testing Problems* (Princeton, New Jersey, Educational Testing Service, 1955), pp. 31-32.

fore rely on the brief samples of behavior provided by tests; thus, a test involves a sample of behavior and a procedure for comparing that behavior with results obtained by other testers.

The accuracy of the predictions, from test behavior to actual life behavior, depends on many factors, including the nature and construction of the test — especially with respect to the concepts of validity and reliability, the conditions under which the tests are given, and the clinical and social sophistication of the examiners.

The concept of validity refers to the degree to which a test instrument actually measures or predicts specific behavior. For example, if intelligence is of specific interest, a desirable test instrument is one that will give an accurate measure of the concept of intelligence as currently defined and accepted. The concept of reliability refers to the consistency of test results over repeated testings: How closely will an individual's test score, or a test score on an alternate version of the same test, approximate the score he obtains on earlier or later testings with the same instrument? From a statistical point of view, reliability is a necessary condition for validity. These concepts will be explored later in greater detail.

THE USES OF TESTS

The purposes of tests are many, but generally tests are used to provide information for decision making. Cronbach has suggested that "the value of test information should be judged by how much it improves decisions over the best possible decisions made without the test."* He points out that if one desires to predict school grades, the information obtained from a scholastic aptitude test will not provide any greater accuracy than previous school grades. School grades can be predicted most accurately, however, using scholastic aptitude tests and previous grades. Generally speaking, then, tests provide additional information or information that is not otherwise easily obtained.

---

*Cronbach, pp. 31-32.

Test information assists in making two types of decisions: institutional and individual. The purposes of decision making create the major difference between these two categories.

Institutional Decisions

Institutions make decisions according to their goals rather than the goals and wishes of the individual. Decisions are made from the perspective of the operation and maintenance of the institution. For example, school personnel typically make institutional decisions concerning possible admission of students into college or special training programs. Test results usually affect those decisions. Similarly, the Army uses tests to assess aptitudes and skills to place personnel in special assignments or training programs.

Industries, schools, and social service agencies typically make institutional decisions in similar ways. Parole boards, for example, decide whether or not to release prisoners. To the extent that parole boards attempt to predict offenders' behaviors and to select only those who exhibit the least potential for antisocial behavior, they engage in institutional decision making. Similarly, probation officers and judges attempt to select good risks for probation. A "good risk" is defined as someone whose potential for repeating his offense is thought to be minimal. In such cases, information is not always complete enough to allow the probation officer or judge to make an intelligent decision. A test's value lies in its potential to provide greater accuracy in decision making than the best possible decisions made without test information.

Individual Decisions

Individual decisions pertain to unique and personal conditions. They are those a person makes about some aspect of his or her own life: the determination of a career, whether or not to enter a special training program or to go to college, the selection of a potential mate. In the social services, individual decisions may be made from the perspective of the person involved.

Under certain conditions, for example, the social worker will make a decision for the client.

There are several ways test information can be utilized in individual decision making. Vocational and aptitude tests commonly are used to help people make career choices. Numbers of young people often wonder which career best suits them or offers them the best chance of success. Frequently, vocational-interest and aptitude batteries allow them to focus on areas of interest with high success potential.

MISUSES OF TESTS

Many counselors tend to rely too heavily on test information. As a result they may seriously limit the options available to an individual. The authors have observed a number of persons who sought college preparation in social work simply because their high school counselors told them they had high scores in this area on a vocational interest test. One student decided to enter the field because of her high score on a vocational interest battery; social work was the specific field mentioned. On close examination, however, her interests and aptitudes did not support her test score, personal commitments, or her common sense. We also have talked with students who decided not to pursue particular programs in higher education because they had low test scores, despite the fact that in at least two such instances the students had achieved commendable previous records of academic success.

Research has demonstrated that success in academic programs predicts future academic success better than test scores. Thus, it would seem that a major decision made on the basis of a test score alone is undesirable.

Tests facilitate decisions; they provide supplementary information for those who make the decisions. An institutional or individual decision made on the basis of a single test score alone is a gross misuse and a misunderstanding of the purposes and limitations of tests. Tests merely sample behavior at any given time and place and, as such, are subject to various errors. Consequently, in many cases test scores and interpretations are insufficient tools and should not be relied on exclusively. The reader is urged to utilize *all the available information* in making any kind of decision.

CHAPTER 2

CLASSIFICATION OF TESTS

TESTS can be classified in a variety of ways — according to structure, purpose, and method of administration. They may be objective or subjective, highly structured or unstructured, designed for administration to groups or individuals. Tests employed in clinical practice include those that measure or predict intelligence, achievement, aptitudes, interests, and personality traits. There are other special diagnostic tests used frequently to assess some particular limitation or potential, e.g. those especially designed to measure the nature and severity of certain types of reading or learning disabilities and those disabilities imposed by organic deterioration or damage. Some tests measure talents inherent to artistic or musical productivity. Intelligence tests probably have the longest and most comprehensive history in clinical, industrial, and academic settings, owing, perhaps, to the belief long held in

Western society that achievement and productivity correlate highly with a concept known as intelligence, controversies regarding the nature of which have raged for thousands of years.

Since direct social service practitioners are likely to be most concerned with a test's intended purpose, a classification of tests was developed as follows:

1. Achievement and aptitude tests, including intelligence tests
2. Personality and interest tests
3. Special diagnostic tests

Considerable confusion exists concerning distinctions between intelligence, achievement, and aptitude. The crux of the argument is whether intelligence as a specific concept can be separated from other factors such as previous learning, achievement, and special kinds of aptitudes. Most theorists today would argue that intelligence tests, aptitude tests, and achievement tests sample and measure various aspects of the same thing. For example, Wechsler, who authored several intelligence tests, defined intelligence as "the aggregate or global capacity of the individual to act purposefully and think rationally and to deal effectively with his environment."* Others argue that intelligence is a function of the total personality and cannot be separated from other aspects of the personality. Wesman, however, advocates perhaps the most comprehensive and one of the most generally accepted definitions of intelligence in the literature: "Intelligence ... is a summation of learning experiences."† This definition recognizes that when measuring intelligence the results of many learning experiences and diverse performances are sampled. Wesman's definition, by implication, does away with artificial distinctions between intelligence, aptitude, and achievement tests. He contends that all of these devices measure what the individual has learned. The difference in labeling merely signifies the different purposes for which the tests will be used. This can be clarified by consid-

---

*David Wechsler, *The Measurement and Appraisal of Adult Intelligence,* 4th ed. (Baltimore, Williams and Wilkins, 1958), p. 7.
†Alexander G. Wesman. "Intelligence Testing," *American Psychologist,* 23:267, 1968.

ering each of the three separate categories: intelligence tests, aptitude tests, and achievement tests.

ACHIEVEMENT AND APTITUDE TESTS, INCLUDING INTELLIGENCE TESTS

Intelligence Tests

Intelligence tests constitute a highly specialized field with a vast body of literature and research surrounding their use. Many varieties of intelligence tests are in use. Each test reflects the specific definition of intelligence and personality-theory commitment of the author. Some tests include only verbal material; others contain much nonverbal material. Some stress problem solving, while others emphasize memory. Certain intelligence tests result in a single total score, e.g. I.Q., whereas others yield several scores or subscores plus a total score.

Varying emphases lead to different test results. One should expect to find some variance in the intelligence test scores of the same person who is examined with different tests. In each test, measures of different kinds of abilities are obtained. It would be surprising if several intelligence tests produced similar test results.

For most purposes, intelligence tests are considered measures of general learning or scholastic aptitude and are most useful in predicting achievement in school, college, or training programs.

Aptitude Tests

Aptitude tests also attempt to measure an individual's potential for achievement. They focus on more circumscribed varieties of achievement, however, than do intelligence tests in determining whether an individual has the potential for achievement in a specifically defined area; for example, an individual's artistic or mechanical aptitude may be measured. Although intelligence correlates to a degree with aptitude and achievement, studies have shown that high intelligence does not necessarily guarantee astuteness or potential in certain areas. Recent data show that intelligence as generally defined does not correlate highly with creativity, especially in the artistic sense, as has been supposed. It is not uncommon to observe individuals who appear extremely intelligent in the traditional sense of the word but who simply do not seem to possess or have developed certain aptitudes. Witness the college professor or physician who is a whiz in the classroom or operating room but who is helpless when faced with an ailing carburetor.

An aptitude test uses a sample of behavior to predict future performance in some specific occupation or training program.

In general use are two major types of aptitude tests: (1) broad-range aptitude test batteries to sample general aptitudes and (2) specific aptitude tests to sample special aptitudes such as music, mathematics, and art.

The most widely used broad-range batteries are the Differential Aptitude Tests (DAT), for high school students, and the General Aptitude Test Battery (GATB), currently used by the United States Employment Service. In addition, a myriad of multiscore aptitude test batteries exists.

Aptitude tests often are employed in selecting individuals for jobs, special training programs, or scholarships. Primarily, the tests predict an individual's potential for achievement in specific occupations or endeavors.

Achievement Tests

Achievement tests, although in many ways similar to intelligence tests, generally are designed to determine what an individual actually has achieved in a certain area of endeavor. They are used to measure a person's present level of knowledge or competence in subjects such as mathematics, science, reading, chemistry, etc. Many achievement tests, unlike other tests, are not standardized but are produced locally. For example, teachers normally develop achievement tests to determine mastery of course material. Thus, an achievement test examines a person's success in past or present study; in contrast, aptitude tests forecast degree of success in some future study. Achievement tests, most widely used in academic settings, usually are reported in the form of grade levels or similar measures of comparison.

PERSONALITY AND INTEREST TESTS

Personality and interest tests focus on what a person typically does or might do in a given situation. What personality and interest tests measure, in contrast with intelligence or achievement tests, is far less clearly defined. Here a number of terms describe similar kinds of things. Adjustment, personality, temperament, interest, preferences, values, and attitudes — all describe similar, broadly defined attributes. It is difficult to say what a specific personality test score means, even after having given the matter careful consideration.

Personality Tests

Clinical psychologists and others interested in the prediction of human behavior long have favored personality tests. They realize that those patterns of behavior usually referred to as personality have a strong influence on what we do. Personality, for example, can largely determine how people characteristically use or direct their intelligence and special creative aptitudes. Indeed, personality deficits or distortions lead to little constructive use of one's talents. Thus, an assessment of personality is vital to those who attempt to help a person channel his or her efforts toward constructive vocational or social use.

Most personality tests rely on vaguely defined scores and scales that are used inconsistently from one author to the next and are based on an underlying rationale that is not always specified.

Few people agree on a standard classification of personality tests. At least three types of tests, however, are in general use:

1. Objective test batteries are those that are not directly subject to clinical interpretation for initial scoring. The Min-

nesota Multiphasic Personality Inventory (MMPI) and the California Psychological Inventory (CPI) are examples of this type of test.

2. The less commonly used situation test measures performance in complex lifelike or simulated situations and tests special kinds of abilities involving an individual's overall responses to specific situations. Industry commonly uses this type to test leadership abilities. When an individual is assigned a group of persons with whom to work and a specific task to accomplish, he or she is observed in the process of completing the task.

3. Projective tests are designed to elicit subjects' responses to an ambiguous stimulus such as a picture or an inkblot. The response is interpreted and scored on the assumption that the way he or she organizes and responds to unstructured or ambiguous stimuli indicates the way the subject organizes and responds to the world around him or her. Responses are assumed to be projections of the subject's unconscious wishes, attitudes, and values. The scoring method is similar to the psychoanalytic method of dream interpretation. Typical projective tests in wide use are the Rorschach (inkblot) and the Thematic Apperception Test (TAT).

Personality tests are used primarily to predict the behavior of individuals in general and specific situations. They commonly aid in predicting postinstitutional adjustment for persons released from prisons, hospitals, and schools or in predicting the likelihood of marital success or job performance. Test reports sometimes contain terms such as anxiety, ego, libido, cathexis, sublimation, etc. A great deal of controversy surrounds the use of various personality tests, especially regarding their validity and reliability. In general, projective tests are not uniformly accurate in predicting the behavior of individuals in either a specific or general situation; they are accurate when given to individuals who deviate greatly from the norm, and in extreme situations. Although it may be fascinating, a projective test may prove disappointing if used to accurately predict behavior in a way that might be useful to most practitioners.

Interest Tests

Interest tests are specific personality tests used mainly in vocational and educational guidance. They are difficult to separate from aptitude tests, but they are included in the general category of personality tests because they are directed toward things such as predicting a person's potential satisfaction with a given type of work. The two most widely used interest inventories are the Strong-Campbell Interest Inventory (SCII) and the Kuder Preference Record (*see* the following example).

Mr. Williams's scores on the Kuder Preference Record indicate that he is highly interested in science, computational activities, and clerical work. These interests are at the 95th, 91st, and 87th percentiles, respectively. He also demonstrates moderate interest in art and mechanical areas. The latter interests are at the 75th and 70th percentiles. Training areas he may wish to consider, then, are computer programming, computer technology, x-ray technology, laboratory technology, drafting, mechanical drawing, computer systems analysis, electronics technology, radar technology, chemical standards work, industrial standards work, bookkeeping, accounting, printing, etc. As noted earlier, his intellectual level and academic preparation are sufficient for him to be successful in a four-year college or technical program.

Interest tests rely generally on self-reporting techniques and are designed to sample both leisure-time and work-related activities, given specific personality aspects in the area of personal likes and dislikes. They are used to determine the amount of preference a person displays for one activity over another. For example, the inventories typically sample reading interest by asking people if they would prefer to read about adventure, business, science, or romance. Another example, the California Occupational Preference Survey, samples eight interest categories: scientific, technical, outdoor, business, clerical, linguistic, aesthetic, and service-related.

Although the interest inventories are considered separately for analysis, they generally are regarded as special personality measures used specifically to predict occupational, vocational, and educational adjustment. For purposes of classification, however, we may regard them as personality measures that fall under the subcategory of objective testing devices. Most of the interest batteries rely on objectively scored testing methods based on standardized methodologies.

SPECIAL DIAGNOSTIC TESTS

A diverse group of tests developed for specific purposes tends to defy classification. Most such tests were developed to measure specific abilities or disabilities. Some tests diagnose cerebral pathology such as brain lesions or other organic abnormalities. There is disagreement as to how much these tests actually measure underlying pathology or primary causation as contrasted with possible poor learning conditions. For example, the Bender Visual Motor Gestalt Test (BVMGT), sometimes regarded as a test for the diagnosis of possible brain damage, also may be considered as a straightforward ability test. It requires the subject to produce various geometric designs using a pencil and paper. The way in which he or she goes about achieving this task is subject to various scoring procedures. Most examiners agree that the BVMGT basically is a performance test, since the examinee is affected by previous learning. However, there is indication that the BVMGT does some rough screening for identifying persons with possible brain damage.

CHAPTER 3

BASIC TEST CONCEPTS

A KNOWLEDGE of some basic testing concepts, including their construction and utilization, is central to understanding the limitations of various tests. Two concepts constitute the criteria used for judging a test in its totality: reliability and validity.

RELIABILITY

Reliability of a test refers to the consistency of scores obtained by the same individuals when taking the test at different times, when parallel versions of the same test are administered, or when the same test is scored by two or more persons. Inconsistency among the scores is called measurement error. A high degree of reliability is essential to ensure confidence in and utility of test results.

If a test is highly unreliable, it is meaningless for measuring a trait. Moreover, its use as a diagnostic or predictive tool can cause great harm. Suppose a psychologist gives a child an achievement test to determine the grade level in which he or she should be placed. Scores from a reliable test would result in the same grade placement regardless of whether the test is given in the morning or afternoon and administered and/or scored by different psychologists. If the score results indicated different grade placement in different instances, the test would be unreliable and misleading. A test must be highly reliable to be useful.

Factors Affecting Reliability

A number of variables affect test reliability.

TEST LENGTH. Assuming that fatigue does not become a major factor, a longer test (one with more items) generally is more reliable than a shorter test.

17

IRREGULARITY OF TESTING CONDITIONS. Changes in conditions from one testing situation to another will affect test reliability. Failure to follow specific directions for giving the test may reveal a considerable difference in scores obtained from the same test taken by the same person at different times. Extreme differences in physical conditions — overheated, uncomfortable test rooms or poor lighting — also will affect reliability. Other factors such as the examiner's responses, racial differences between the examiner and subject, moods, illness, cheating by the examinee, etc., may threaten test reliability.

SCORER ERROR. When tests are not scored objectively or the details of scoring are ignored, unreliability results. Objective tests reduce the possibilities of scorer error. Tests designed to elicit subjective responses require special training for scoring and are less reliable than objective tests. Indeed, many score errors occur as a result of the examiner's inexperience.

Determining Reliability

Two basic procedures commonly are used to estimate test reliability: the internal-consistency procedure and the alternate-form procedure. The internal-consistency procedure determines statistically to what extent all test items measure the same thing. If all questions within a test measure the same characteristic, the test will be highly reliable. For example, if a test is used to measure math achievement, it is important that all questions measure math ability and not other traits or abilities, e.g. reading ability. The greater the number of questions that do not measure math ability, the lower the obtained reliability will be. The internal-consistency procedure most always is the best estimate of reliability and usually is close to the reliability estimated by the alternate-form procedure.

The alternate-form procedure involves giving an individual two versions of the same test at different times (usually about two weeks apart). Similar scores on the two tests would indicate high test reliability. Dissimilar scores would signify low test reliability or that the characteristic being measured would have changed between tests.

There are other procedures for estimating reliability, although for most situations they are not recommended. The two most common are the test-retest and split-half procedures. The test-retest procedure involves giving the *same* test to the same person on two occasions. The similarity of scores across tests is used to estimate the reliability. A shortcoming of this procedure is that performance on the first test might influence performance on the retest. Answers may be remembered, or associations may occur between tests. In general, the test-retest procedure tends to overestimate a test's reliability and should be avoided.

The split-half procedure involves separating the test into halves, usually odd-numbered items in one half and even-numbered items in the other. The similarity between scores is used to estimate the test's reliability. Actually, the split-half procedure is an estimate of the reliability that can be ascertained from the internal-consistency procedure. The internal-consistency procedure determines to what extent halves of a test measure the same thing. In most situations, the internal-consistency procedure provides a better estimate of reliability.

It should be noted that reliability usually is expressed in the form of a reliability coefficient that indicates the degree of reliability. A reliability coefficient of 1.00 indicates perfect reliability, while a coefficient of .00 indicates a complete lack of reliability. How high a reliability coefficient needs to be before a test is useful is difficult to determine. Generally, a test should have a reliability of .90 when results are used to make applied decisions.

When a test contains several subtests, as in the Wechsler Intelligence Scales, the test as a whole will be more reliable than its separate components. As mentioned earlier, longer tests usually are more reliable than shorter ones. Therefore, the reliability of subtests should be checked if their scores are to be used apart from overall test performance.

A test must be reliable to be useful. The degree of reliability, indicated by a reliability coefficient, can be estimated by different methods. The method used depends on what is being measured, how the test was constructed, and what source of error is being investigated. In nearly all situations, the internal consistency of the test is the best estimate of reliability.

VALIDITY

To make a judgment about the general validity of a test, it is essential that the user of any psychological test information determine what kinds of decisions he or she is going to make regarding the use of that test. In its broad sense, validity denotes the extent to which a test measures or predicts that for which it was designed. In other words, validity is the most basic and perhaps the most important single attribute of a test. If a test is designed to predict occupational success, the extent to which it does so may be said to be a measure of its validity. It is important to recognize, however, that psychological tests may have a high degree of validity for one purpose but almost none for other purposes.

Various measures of validity used in psychological testing include content, predictive, and construct validity. Although much has been written about validity measures, for practical purposes most social service practitioners will concern themselves primarily with predictive validity.

Predictive validity, also called empirical or criterion validity, is established by determining how well a test predicts performance against a specific criterion. A test's predictive validity is determined by operationally defining what the test should do and what outcomes it can predict: The test's success in predicting that outcome is the extent to which the test proves valid. Thus, if a practitioner uses an instrument to screen people for discharge from a correctional institution, how well that instrument predicts specific aspects of postinstitutional adjustment, such as recidivism, determines the test's validity.

Again, validity is determined by a specific definition of what the test should do. It probably is more useful to speak about the validity of a specific *use* of the test rather than about the test *per se*. A test that successfully predicts postinstitutional adjustment and is highly valid for that purpose, for example, might prove ineffective, and therefore invalid, in identifying potential automobile salesmen.

Schools establish predictive validity by using intelligence tests to predict potential achievement. Scores obtained on specific intelligence tests are compared with grades earned in school. In a similar way, the predictions based on occupational preference tests are validated by comparing ratings by individuals and employers at a later data.

Factors Affecting Validity

Two major factors influence predictive validity:

1. The specific criteria used to establish validation may vary from study to study with different scores obtained from each set of criteria. Therefore, it is necessary to carefully consider which criteria are most important for the decision at hand.
2. Some tests are defined more specifically than others in terms of what they are intended to do. For example, easily identified criteria such as school grades can validate a scholastic aptitude test. It is very difficult, if not impossible, however, to establish acceptable criteria for an anxiety scale or a value scale. Where such difficulty in defining criteria related to the intended results of the test exists, high validity cannot be expected.

Practitioners should keep in mind a general rule of thumb: *For a test to have any utility, it must provide accurate information that can help predict behavior.* Thus, the less specific the test objectives are, the less useful the test is in predicting behavior.

Predictive validity generally is reported as a numerical figure called a validity coefficient — a measure of validity achieved by computing a coefficient of correlation between the test and a criterion.

CHAPTER 4

BASIC STATISTICAL CONCEPTS

IN addition to understanding reliability and validity as essential concepts underlying test construction, the consumer of test information should know how test results typically are reported.

NORMS

The familiar expression, "How are you?" and the response, "In relation to what?" best expresses what norms are all about. That is, they provide those standards against which a given value is compared. Norms may be used to determine how well a person does in comparison to other people.

Many people in the social services view test results simply in the form of a raw score. Without more information, it is impossible to use the test results to make a productive decision. For example, the raw score of 65 may mean that sixty-five test items were answered correctly. If there is no norm for comparing that score with other responses, one can attach no meaning to that score. A set of norms is imperative to understand the meaning of raw test scores.

Cronbach has defined a test as "a systematic procedure for comparing the behavior of two or more persons."* In spite of the philosophical difficulties one may have with making comparisons, psychological testing does just this. Norms are accumulated test data for a specified group used to make comparisons between individuals and groups. On some tests, for example, the performance of persons in a specific geographic location is compared with the performance of persons nationally.

It must be perfectly clear to the social service practitioner just how an individual's test results compare with specific responses from other groups. Who or what a person is compared with makes a great difference. Consider the following example: Jane Sloe, a seventeen-year-old inmate in the state correctional institution for girls, received a raw score of 163 on a vocabulary test designed to predict academic success in collegiate programs. At this point, her probation officer must decide whether to release her by September 1 so that she may enter college. Her raw score of 163 means that she did as well or better than —

- 99 percent of the residents of the state school for girls;
- 87 percent of the twelfth grade students in Capital City;
- 83 percent of the entering freshman at State University;
- 75 percent of the graduating seniors at State University;
- 96 percent of the custodial and treatment staff at State School for Girls;
- 15 percent of the faculty in the English Department at State

*L. J. Cronbach, *Essentials of Psychological Testing*, 3rd ed. (New York, Harper & Row Pubs., 1970), p. 21.

University.

Although Jane's absolute performance remains unchanged, the impression of how well she has done may differ considerably as the norm groups change. This extreme illustration points up the importance of specifying the norm group to which a person is compared.

To fully understand a norm group, one must gather as much information as possible describing the norm group and determine how the person tested differs from it. In viewing any norm group, consider such important variables as age, sex, previous education, socioeconomic background, ethnic membership, and occupation. In other words, one should use the most appropriate norm group for the individual examinee and situation.

Publishers supply norm information on most standardized tests, especially educational achievement tests. Most test publishers routinely report norm information and specify if they will make available local and national norm information. In addition, standard test references report norms. Social service practitioners should use this rule of thumb regarding norms: *The more information provided describing the norm group, the more accurately one can assess to what extent a given individual resembles the norm group.*

Test manuals usually provide broadly based or national norms. When using such norms, it is important to obtain more detailed information about the groups used to establish them. Most norm groups will not compose an entire population; they sample what the test constructors consider the relevant population. To establish norms, they divide the relevant population into subgroups that appear in the sample in proportion to their numbers in the population. Ideally, those individuals who compose the sample from each subgroup are selected randomly. Frequently, test constructors subdivide populations according to such characteristics as rural-urban residence, age, sex, race, socioeconomic status, religion, and geographic region. Sometimes they seek to establish from a specific stratified population what they consider to be normal performance ranges. In some cases, however, they may omit certain elements of the population in the original norming groups and thereby render the specific test irrelevant for use on that population. For example, one of the most frequent criticisms of intelligence tests is that adequate samples of American Indians were not included in the original norming group. Such tests, like the Wechsler Intelligence Scales, may provide a poor basis for comparing the performance of American Indians with other segments of the population.

Social service practitioners, then, must focus on the detailed description of the norm group's relevant characteristics. Furthermore, when subgroup differences are known to be related to test performances, it is important to report separate norms for the subgroups. A case in point involves the effects of early child-rearing practices and development in multilingual homes. A test that focuses on the development of English vocabulary, standardized on a population of Midwestern school children, may not be a valid basis for comparing the performance of Southwestern Chicano children who come from Spanish-speaking homes. Again, it may be desirable and even necessary to establish separate norms for people from a similar population before meaningful comparisons are made. One must remember that how accurately a norm group represents the population to be tested is more essential than the absolute size of that norm group. The larger the sample, the more stable the statistics based on the sample, but a representative norm group of moderate size is much more useful than a large, poorly defined group.

MEASURES OF POSITION

Numbers that tell us where a score value stands within a set of scores are measures of position. There are two commonly used measures of position: rank and percentile rank.

Rank is the simplest description of position. It designates the highest, the next highest, the third highest, and so on, to the lowest — a simple way of describing the position of a person or a score with respect to a distribution of scores. However, rank designation is limited, i.e. its interpretation depends on the size of the group. It generally is used in an informal sense, such as designating a person's standing in his or her high school graduating class; however, the meaning of graduating first in a class of three is not as clear as graduating first in a class of 5,000.

Percentile rank states a person's relative position within a defined group. Thus, a percentile rank of 97 indicates a score as high or higher than those made by 97 percent of the people in a particular group. Percentile ranks are one of the most widely used measures of position for reporting test scores, especially on scholastic achievement tests. Although easily understood and commonly used, percentile ranks have a major limitation: They are based on the number of people with scores higher or lower than the specified score value. Percentile ranks tend to obscure all information about distribution of scores and the absolute differences in raw scores achieved by individuals. This information can be obtained by focusing on other measures of variability and central tendency.

MEASURES OF CENTRAL TENDENCY

A measure of central tendency is a representative common denominator for a set of scores. One of the most widespread statistical evaluative statements in regard to a person's ability or test performance is based on comparing that performance or score to a measure of central tendency. People can be classified as above-average skiers, below-average dancers, or average fly fishermen; amazingly, such statements usually are accepted as meaningful and accurate. What the person means by average frequently is not defined, and the norm group to which the person is being compared rarely is defined. To be useful, reports of test results must be precise. For instance, a single score can be above or below average, depending on the measure of central tendency being used to describe average. Also, as implied earlier, a person can be above or below average, depending on the norm group with which he or she is being compared. An individual may be below average in snow skiing when compared to skiers in Boise, Idaho, but above average when compared to skiers in Selma, Alabama.

Three measurements of central tendency are in general use: the arithmetic mean, the median, and the mode. Each measure can be used to represent a point of central tendency or the average of a distribution of scores.

Mean

The mean, or arithmetic mean, is the most common and useful measure of central tendency. The mean of a distribution of scores is the sum of all the scores divided by the number of scores in the distribution. It is the measurement that is most often thought of as the average. It has mathematical qualities that make it useful with other statistics, and in almost every situation it is the central tendency measure of choice.

Median

Another way of indicating central tendency is to locate that point in a distribution that divides it into two equal parts, that is, the point with 50 percent of the scores above it and 50 percent below it. A score occurring at the median would be the 50th percentile rank or 50th centile. The median rather than the mean frequently is used when distributions are highly asymmetric — when the shape of the distribution below the mean is highly different from the distribution's shape above the mean. Standardized tests most always have symmetrical distributions representing normative data, so then the mean is seen much more often than the median.

Mode

The mode is the score in an interval with the highest frequency. It is the simplest measure of central tendency and is used only when a very quick estimate is needed or when the most typical score is sought. With the exception of these two situations, the mode probably should not be used.

MEASURES OF VARIABILITY

Comparing a test score only with the mean of a distribution indicates whether it is above or below the mean. It does not give additional information about the score's position in comparison to other scores in its relative position, i.e. other scores above or below the mean. Knowing that a person scored 110 on a test with a mean of 100 indicates only that the score is above the mean. If the scores are diffused, e.g. from 10 to 190, it would appear to be close to the mean. If the distribution of scores shows little variability, e.g. 85 to 115, a score of 110 might be considerably above the mean.

To interpret an individual test score, two measures of the distribution of test scores must be available: a measure of central tendency and a measure of variability. That is, what was the average score and how diffused were the scores? Using both measures, the position of an individual score relative to other scores on the same test will be clear. Three measures of variability in widespread use are the standard deviation, the semi-interquartile range, and the range.

Standard Deviation

Standard deviation is the most widely used and dependable measure of variability because it fits mathematically with other statistics; thus, it becomes the basis for a number of other statistical measures, including standard scores. It is used as a measure of variability in situations where the mean is used as a measure of central tendency, and it is sensitive to how far each score in a distribution varies from the mean of that distribution. The standard deviation is the square root of the mean of the squared deviations from the mean (of a distribution). The standard deviation generally is represented either by the Greek symbol δ or the letter s. For all practical purposes, $s = \delta = $ standard deviation.

The standard deviation is used to make interpretations of the variability of scores in a distribution (Table I lists some of the characteristics of standard deviation). In a normal distribution of scores, 34 percent of the scores lie between the mean and a point that is one standard deviation on either side of the mean. Thus, 68 percent of the scores on that distribution will be dispersed between a point that is one standard deviation below the mean. Approximately 14 percent of the scores in a normal distribution fall between a point that is one standard deviation away from the mean in the same direction. Therefore, as illustrated in Table I, approximately 96 percent (14 + 34 + 34 + 14) of all scores will fall within two standard deviations ± of the mean. The importance of standard deviation will become clearer when standard scores and errors of measurement and estimation are discussed.

Semi-interquartile Range

The semi-interquartile range is a measure of the dispersion represented by the middle half of a distribution. In other words, the semi-interquartile range represents one-half the distance between the 25th and 75th percentiles on a distribution. The semi-interquartile range is preferred to the standard deviation in the same situations where the median is preferred over the mean — namely, when the distribution is radically asymmetric.

Range

The range simply is the difference between the highest and lowest scores in a distribution. It is used as a measure of variability in situations where the mode is used as a measure of central tendency. Although it is the easiest measure of variability to compute, it also gives the least information. The range should be used only when there is specific interest in the most extreme scores in a distribution.

RAW SCORES AND STANDARD SCORES

The direct numerical report of a person's score is called a raw score. This score may represent the number of problems correct,

TABLE I

COMPARISON OF SOME STANDARD SCORES

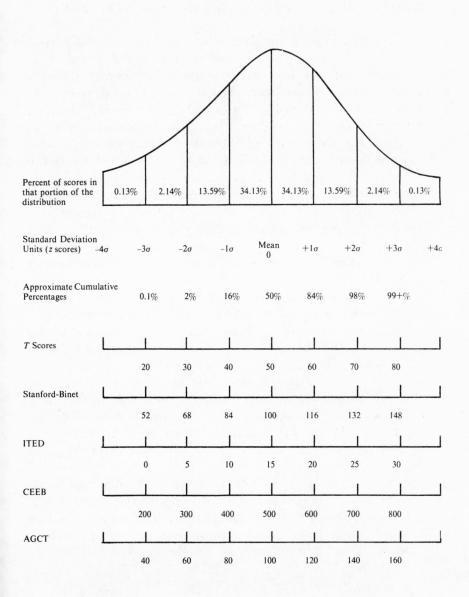

Percent of scores in that portion of the distribution	0.13%	2.14%	13.59%	34.13%	34.13%	13.59%	2.14%	0.13%

| Standard Deviation Units (z scores) | -4σ | -3σ | -2σ | -1σ | Mean 0 | $+1\sigma$ | $+2\sigma$ | $+3\sigma$ | $+4\sigma$ |

| Approximate Cumulative Percentages | 0.1% | 2% | 16% | 50% | 84% | 98% | 99+% |

| T Scores | 20 | 30 | 40 | 50 | 60 | 70 | 80 |

| Stanford-Binet | 52 | 68 | 84 | 100 | 116 | 132 | 148 |

| ITED | 0 | 5 | 10 | 15 | 20 | 25 | 30 |

| CEEB | 200 | 300 | 400 | 500 | 600 | 700 | 800 |

| AGCT | 40 | 60 | 80 | 100 | 120 | 140 | 160 |

the amount of time required to complete a test, or any other numerical value representing test performance. Raw scores are misunderstood easily because they do not provide a basis for comparison with other test scores. To compare test scores, a common scale of measurement, including a measure of central tendency and a measure of variability, must be applied to all scores.

The most common standard scores are based on the *z score*, which has a mean of 0 and a standard deviation of 1. Therefore, a *z* score indicates how many standard deviations above or below the mean a raw score lies. For instance, a *z* score of +2.00 is located two standard deviations above the mean, while a *z* score of −2.00 is located two standard deviations below the mean. The *z* score gives useful information that a raw score does not. As shown in Table I, a *z* score can be transformed into a centile. The approximate cumulative percentages are represented below the row indicating *z* scores. A *z* score of +2.00 is directly above the 98th percent cumulative percentage and, therefore, corresponds to the 98th centile. A *z* score of +1.00 is equal to the 84th centile because approximately 84 percent of all scores in the distribution fall below it. A *z* of 0 corresponds to the 50th centile.

If the standard deviation and the mean of a distribution of scores are known, raw scores can easily be transformed to *z* scores. The Stanford-Binet has a mean of 100 and a standard deviation of 15. Therefore, a score of 100 is equal to a *z* score of 0 and a centile of 50; 115 equals a *z* score of +1.00 and a centile of 84. To convert any raw score to a *z* score, subtract the mean of the distribution and divide the answer by the distribution's standard deviation, i.e. $z = $ (Raw Score −Mean)/ Standard Deviation. For a Stanford-Binet score of 130, the corresponding *z* score is +2.00 [$z = (130-100/15$] and the centile is 98.

Although *z* scores yield much information, they have some shortcomings in practice: The negative numbers are a nuisance, and the standard deviation unit (1) is small. To make standard deviation units larger, each number can be multiplied by a constant. To eliminate negative numbers, a constant can be added to the resultant number. The added constant and multiplied constant become the new mean and standard deviation, respectively. For instance, to change z scores to T scores (*see* Table I), each z score is multiplied by 10, and 50 is added to each answer. Therefore, T scores have a mean of 50 and a standard deviation of 10. A z score of +1.00 equals a T score of 60 $[T = 10(z) + 50]$ and a centile of 84.

A frequently encountered test based on a standard score is the *College Entrance Examination Board (CEEB)*, administered by the Education Testing Service. The CEEB was standardized in 1941 on a population of college applicants. Using the scores based on the applicants of 1941, the testers have developed the CEEB as follows: The mean of the test is 500, and the standard deviation is 100. With this information in mind, the test user can estimate the relative position of any given score. For example, a score of 800 on the CEEB is three standard deviations above the mean. This means that the examinee achieved a higher score than more than 99 percent of the population on whom the test was standardized.

It is essential to remember that (1) most standard scores are based on the properties of the normal curve, and (2) standard scores generally include such information as the mean and the standard deviation of the distribution.

PLACEMENT SCORES

The most common score used in reporting performance on standardized achievement tests for school children is the grade-placement score, which resembles the age scores. It is found by determining the average score of school students at a corresponding grade placement. Grade-placement scores generally are stated in tenths of a school year; for example, 6.2 refers to the second month of grade six. This approach assumes that children learn relatively uniformly throughout the school year but that no learning occurs during the summer vacation — an assumption not necessarily true. Grade-placement scores, however, often are used to estimate where a person should be placed in school-related work.

MEASURES OF CORRELATION

Measures of correlation estimate how closely two or more variables are related to each other. Variables can be related in a positive or negative direction. A positive correlation indicates that as one variable increases, the other increases. A negative correlation indicates that as one variable increases, the other decreases. For instance, height and weight are related positively. In general, the taller people are, the more they weigh. Scores on I.Q. tests and achievement in school also are positively related; students who score high on I.Q. tests tend to be higher achievers academically than students with low I.Q. scores. Conversely, the size of car engines and gas mileage are negatively related; larger engines tend to get lower gas mileages than smaller engines.

One reason that relationships between variables are important is because one variable can be predicted from another. Weight can be predicted from height, school achievement can be predicted from I.Q. scores, and gas mileage can be predicted from engine size. How accurately one variable can be predicted from another depends on the strength of the relationship between them. The stronger the relationship, the more accurately one can be predicted from the other.

The strength of association between variables is estimated by a numerical index called the correlation coefficient. A correlation coefficient expresses — in numerical values that range from +1.00 (a perfect positive relationship), to .00 (no relationship), to −1.00 (a perfect negative relationship) — the strength of relationship between variables. The only time one variable can be predicted with complete accuracy from another is when the relationship is perfect (a correlation of +1.00 or −1.00). Unfortunately, psychological tests are not perfectly correlated with behaviors being predicted. For instance, the relationship between I.Q. scores and school achievement generally produces correlation coefficients of +.50. Although I.Q. scores do not allow perfect prediction of school achievement, they predict well enough to be highly useful.

As discussed earlier, how well a test predicts behavior for

which it was intended is called the *predictive validity* of the test. A correlation coefficient between the test scores and the criterion being predicted indicates the usefulness of the test for that purpose and is called a *validity coefficient*. The higher the coefficient, the more valid the use of the test and the more accurate the predictions. It should be noted that the sign of the relationship (positive or negative) indicates the direction — not strength — of the relationship. A correlation of −.50 between a test and predicted behavior indicates the same degree of usefulness (validity) as a correlation of +.50.

ESTIMATES OF MEASUREMENT AND PREDICTIVE ERROR

Psychological tests are not perfectly reliable or valid. Errors are made in measuring and in predicting subsequent behavior. Both types of errors can be estimated statistically.

Consistent test results cannot be expected, because psychological tests are not perfectly reliable. Owing to *chance factors*, a person probably would not receive exactly the same score if he or she took the same test at different times during the day, if the test were administered by different persons, or if the test were taken in one location as opposed to another. How much the scores could be expected to vary is estimated by the standard error of measurement (SEM). The SEM estimates how far a person's *obtained score* deviates from the *true score* on a test, that is, how much variability can be expected owing to chance factors. On an achievement test, the true score would be an estimate of what the person actually knows, while the obtained score would be the score he or she actually received.

Table II illustrates approximately how close an obtained I.Q. can be expected to be to a true I.Q. if the SEM is 3. The hypothetical distribution, a normal curve, represents error scores (Obtained I.Q. − True I.Q.) for several hundred cases. Since the errors are the result of chance factors, sometimes the obtained I.Q. would be higher than the true I.Q. (+ side of the distribution), and sometimes it would be lower (− side of the distribution). The SEM represents one standard deviation on the

TABLE II

ILLUSTRATIONS OF THE STANDARD ERROR OF MEASUREMENT AND STANDARD ERROR OF ESTIMAT

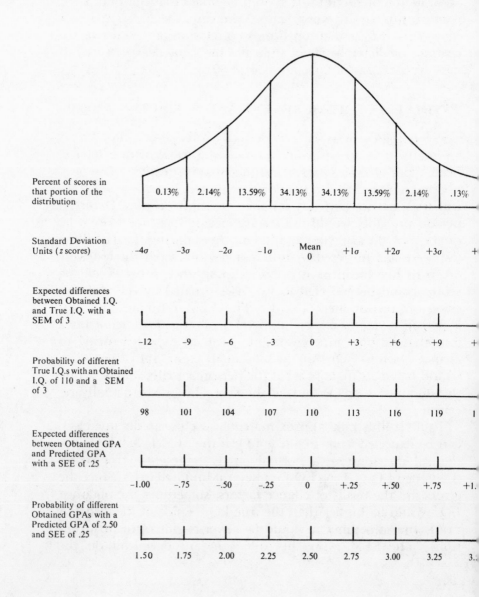

Percent of scores in that portion of the distribution	0.13%	2.14%	13.59%	34.13%	34.13%	13.59%	2.14%	.13%
Standard Deviation Units (*z* scores)	-4σ	-3σ	-2σ	-1σ	Mean 0	$+1\sigma$	$+2\sigma$	$+3\sigma$	+
Expected differences between Obtained I.Q. and True I.Q. with a SEM of 3	-12	-9	-6	-3	0	$+3$	$+6$	$+9$	+
Probability of different True I.Q.s with an Obtained I.Q. of 110 and a SEM of 3	98	101	104	107	110	113	116	119	1
Expected differences between Obtained GPA and Predicted GPA with a SEE of .25	-1.00	$-.75$	$-.50$	$-.25$	0	$+.25$	$+.50$	$+.75$	+1.
Probability of different Obtained GPAs with a Predicted GPA of 2.50 and SEE of .25	1.50	1.75	2.00	2.25	2.50	2.75	3.00	3.25	3.

distribution-of-error scores. With a SEM of 3, 68 percent of the time the obtained I.Q. will be within ± 3 points of the true I.Q., and 96 percent of the time it will be within 6 points of the true I.Q. The more reliable the test, the smaller the SEM is. With an obtained I.Q. of 110 and a SEM of 3, one could be 68 percent confident that the true I.Q. lies between 107 and 113 and 96 percent confident that it lies between 104 and 116 (*see* Table II). When making practical decisions about people from tests, the SEM should be taken into account.

The standard error of estimate (SEE) is one of the most important statistics to understand when predicting behavior from tests. It estimates how well a behavior can be predicted from a test by indicating how much error can be expected. Suppose an aptitude test is used to predict a student's grade point average (GPA) in a nursing program at a local college. The test results yield a prediction that the student will obtain a 2.8 GPA in the program. The student is very pleased but wants to know how accurate the prediction will be: is he or she likely to receive a 2.0 or 3.5 GPA?

The SEE represents one standard deviation on a distribution-of-error scores (obtained score – predicted score). Table II illustrates how close a predicted GPA can be expected to be to an obtained GPA with a SEE of .25. Like the SEM, the SEE represents one standard deviation on a normal distribution-of-error scores. In some cases, the obtained GPA would be higher than the predicted GPA (+ side of the distribution), and sometimes it would be lower (– side of the distribution). With a predicted GPA of 2.5 and a SEE of .25, the following statements could be made. The obtained GPA will be between 2.25 and 2.75 (+ to– I.Q. and + to – .25 GPA) 68 percent of the time, while 96 percent of the time the obtained GPA will be between 2.00 and 3.00 (+ to – I.Q. and + to – .50 GPA). According to the predicted GPA and SEE, the probability of an obtained GPA above 3.00 or below 2.00 is 4 percent (*see* Table II).

It should be noted that the SEE, as discussed above, is used only when a highly quantifiable behavior such as GPA is being predicted. In some situations, less precise categorical predictions, e.g. pass versus fail, are made. When categorical predictions are made, the probabilities of such predictions being correct should be furnished if possible. In other situations, the predicted behavior, e.g. anxious or depressed, is difficult to quantify, and general statements, e.g. the client will tend to be depressed, will have to suffice. Usually, the more quantified the predicted behavior, the more useful it will be.

CHAPTER 5

LIMITATIONS OF TESTS

SUPPLEMENTARY MEASURES

THE full assessment of a person's abilities, disabilities, and various personal qualities requires a progressive type of approach. Since a test simply is a behavior sample to be regarded cautiously, it follows that test scores are minimal estimates of behavior and abilities. Broad-spectrum tests like the Wechsler Intelligence Scales are initial steps to assessing general ability. When a social service worker must make an important decision, he or she should move through progressive stages of assessment using test information that deals with specific intellectual, perceptual, and/or cognitive factors. Existing tests can provide only clues and rough estimates regarding an individual's abilities and capacities. *The results of any one test should be viewed cautiously.*

TEST CONSTRUCTION LIMITS

One of the major difficulties in deciding how to best use the various kinds of test results springs from uncertainty about what tests actually measure. Some are designed to measure verbal learning and abstractions, while others assess manual skill potential. The Wechsler and Stanford-Binet originally were constructed to measure performance and verbal factors. Yet many psychologists agree that the weighting of the Stanford-Binet is more toward measuring verbal ability than are the Wechsler tests, which strike a more even balance between verbal and performance items. A person's achievement on verbal or performance tests partially reflects previous learning experiences. Thus other factors, all related to previous exposure to similar materials, are important determinants for assessing test limitations.

Factors such as membership in specific geographic groups are related to mastery of subject content. For example, urban residents are exposed to a more diverse range of people-related stimuli than are rural residents. A rural resident may define an elevator as a grain storage facility, while an urban resident may describe it as a device used to move people up and down in a building. If this were a test question, i.e. define an elevator, standardized on an urban population, the rural resident's answer might be judged unacceptable. Such a question will not fairly measure his or her potential ability to acquire knowledge. Similarly, many achievement and ability tests do not sample fairly the potential abilities of members of various ethnic groups.

EFFECTS OF CULTURE

For a test to be truly fair, all of the examinees should have had an equal opportunity to acquire the needed background. There have been many attempts to construct culture-free or culture-fair tests — those that supposedly do not depend on previous experience — but most social scientists believe that experience affects all behavior.

Cultural factors affect test performance. Previous training experiences influence outcome. The Zuni Indians are taught cooperation rather than competition, and so the performance of a Zuni Indian on a competitive test might vary considerably from that of a person reared in a culture that stresses competition. Some tests may exhibit a cultural bias simply because the examinee is not familiar with the testing materials.

Heredity versus Environment

The most historically prominent controversy regarding culture and testing concerns the interaction of culture and heredity in determining measured intelligence. The controversy was rekindled in 1969 when Arthur Jensen wrote an article for the prestigious *Harvard Educational Review,* suggesting that intellectual development was determined primarily by genetic transmission.* The dominant hypothesis prior to Jensen's work suggested that intelligence largely was determined by environmental experiences. Evidence on both sides of this important controversy is reviewed in the following sections of this chapter.

Jensen's thesis rests on the correlations between the intelligence test scores of identical and fraternal twins reared together and apart. For identical twins, i.e. twins having all genes in common, reared in the same home environment the average correlation is a high +.89, whereas fraternal twins, i.e. twins having 50 percent of genes in common, reared in the same environment yield an average correlation of +.50. When comparable correlations are computed for groups of twins separated at birth and reared in different environments, the relationships drop to +.45 for identical twins and +.30 for fraternal twins. The important point is that regardless of the environmental circumstances, identical twins maintain a greater similarity in measured I.Q. However, these data reveal that environmental factors apparently also are involved in the determination of intellectual development. From the above findings, Jensen con-

---

*A. R. Jensen. "How Much Can We Boost I.Q. and Scholastic Achievement?" *Harvard Educational Review* (Winter 1969), pp. 1-123.

cluded that 80 percent of the variability in I.Q. test scores stems from genetic determinants, 10 percent is related to environmental stimulation, and the remaining 10 percent comes from measurement error.

Opinion is divided regarding Jensen's estimations. In fact, some prominent investigators currently believe that environmental stimulation is the dominant force in determining intellectual growth. There is evidence, for example, that animals receiving social and physical stimulation early in life show higher scores on measures of animal intelligence than their nonstimulated counterparts. Moreover, these differences stem from actual chemical and structural changes in the brain that apparently are caused by the stimulation.* On the human level, numerous well-controlled studies indicate that environmental stimulation can improve measured I.Q., particularly when the stimulation occurs within the first few years of life.†

One outgrowth of the nature-versus-nurture controversy concerns speculations regarding I.Q. differences among racial groups. For instance, black persons in the United States score on the average fifteen points below whites on intelligence assessments. If one were to follow Jensen's argument, the conclusion might be that blacks are genetically inferior to whites in terms of measured I.Q. Such a hypothesis ignores (1) findings that the high verbal component of I.Q. tests tends to attenuate the performance of blacks and (2) data indicating the importance of environmental factors in the growth and measurement of intelligence. Concerning the latter point, it has been found that in the investigation of children of mixed (black-white) marriages, the children's I.Q.s tended to vary in accordance with the race of the caretaker (usually the mother). If the mother was black, the child's I.Q. would tend to be toward the mean of the black population (about 85). If the mother was white, the child's I.Q. usually was closer to the mean for whites

---

*M. R. Rosenzweig, E. L. Bennett, and M. C. Diamond, "Brain Changes in Response to Experience," in *The Nature and Nurture of Behavior* (San Francisco, W. H. Freeman & Co., 1973).

†M. Kodak and H. M. Skeels. "A Follow-up Study of One Hundred Adopted Children," *Journal of Genetic Psychology*, 75:85-125, 1949.

(about 100).* The results suggest that white mothers are more likely to convey to a child information and experiences that will be valuable vis-à-vis performance on intelligence tests.

The research regarding the relative contributions of heredity and environment indicates that the *safest* position is one of the interaction; that is, nature and nurture combine in complex ways to determine intelligence. Unless future research indicates the contrary, it probably is best to use an environmental perspective with respect to racial differences. The I.Q. tests assume that every test taker has had equal opportunity to learn correct responses to intelligence test items. In our society, in the case of blacks, other minority groups, and, indeed, some white persons, the assumption probably is not valid.

It is interesting to note that lawsuits are pending in some areas to eliminate the use of I.Q. testing in assigning children to special education programs. The suits contend that because of different cultural backgrounds the tests favor white, middle-class children and discriminate against minorities.

OTHER LIMITATIONS

It should be kept in mind that the *performance of any individual on a test simply is a sample of behavior,* and, as such, performance on any one test is a minimal estimate. Naturally, the more measures of similar variables, the more reliance one can place on such estimates, but any contradictory scores on two or more tests that measure similar attributes should be noted. If such a contradication exists, one should seek professional interpretation of the differences. At least three variables may be involved: the tests themselves, the individual or group being tested, and the conditions of test administration.

---

*L. Willerman, A. F. Naylor, and N. C. Myrianthopoulis. "Intellectual Development of Children from Interracial Matings," *Science, 170*:1329-1331, 1970.

CHAPTER 6

HOW TO MAKE A TEST REFERRAL

MOST social service personnel should make test referrals as a routine part of their work. The best test referrals identify the specific information sought.

Since testing should have as its major purpose the provision of useful information for decision making, the psychologist who selects a test that will provide such information needs to know what kinds of decisions the social service worker must make and what kinds of information are available about the client. Following is a suggested guide for making test referrals.

Suggested Guide for Test Referrals

1. Reason for referral — what kind of information is wanted and what kinds of decisions will be made (or attempted). (Theoretical terms should be avoided, e.g. Does he have an

oedipal conflict?)
  2. Description of the subject, including —
  a. age
  b. sex
  c. education
  d. occupation and employment history
  e. ethnic membership and experience
  f. special disabilities, handicaps, or physical abnormalities.
  3. The results of any previous testing, if available, including testing dates, scores, and test names.
  4. A brief history of the subject's involvement with the agency.
  5. A brief statement of any case-management plans suitable for the subject.

Given this information, a competent examiner should be able to select the tests that will best provide the information the social service worker needs. The examiner also should be able to interpret the test results in a way that is useful in making specific case-management decisions.

Some Hints for Dealing with Psychologists

If the resultant test report is in a form that is difficult to use in decision making, one should ask the examiner for a consultation or interpretation. It should be remembered, however, that what is acquired from such a meeting depends largely on the questions asked. It is advisable to key the questions to specific decisions about the subject; for example, Will Johnny get through college at State University? or, Is there a possibility that Johnny may commit suicide?

Although no examiner can answer either question with certainty, he or she can provide some information about the probability of either event occurring. Ethical examiners also will provide the necessary explanations about the limitation of the instrument.

The social service worker should prepare persons referred for psychological tests for the actual examination procedure. Such preparation should include an explanation of why the referral was made and a description of what can be expected in the testing situation — how long it will take, where it will be done, etc. This information can be obtained on request from the examiner.

It generally is not appropriate to request the examiner to administer a specific test. The test selection should be left to his or her discretion unless an exception can be justified.

Many test reports contain much technical jargon, but one can ask examiners to explain in a test report all terms that are not understood. Technical jargon is meant for other psychologists and frequently does not convey a great deal of meaning to test-information users.

Psychological examiners have no magical powers. The same information resulting from a psychological examination might well come from others in everyday situations. People who have known the subject for a time and have observed him or her in different situations often can reveal more about the subject than most examiners. It should be remembered that tests sample only a limited domain of behavior; what happens in real-life situations may be the most important single predictor of future behavior.

CHAPTER 7

COMMONLY USED TESTS

THERE are hundreds of psychological tests currently in use. The tests presented here have been restricted to those with which social service practitioners are most likely to come in contact. They compose the tests commonly used to provide some of the answers that social service practitioners often need. The tests are presented in three groups (as explained in Chapter 2):

1. Achievement and Aptitude Tests, including Intelligence Tests
2. Personality and Interest Tests
3. Special Diagnostic Tests

Tests within each group are presented in alphabetical order.

ACHIEVEMENT AND APTITUDE TESTS, INCLUDING INTELLIGENCE TESTS

General Aptitude Test Battery (GATB)
Goodenough-Harris Drawing Test (Draw-A-Man Test)
Otis Self-Administering Test of Mental Ability
Peabody Picture Vocabulary Test (PPVT)
Stanford-Binet Scale
Vineland Social Maturity Scale
Wechsler Adult Intelligence Scale (WAIS)
Wechsler Intelligence Scale for Children (WISC)
Wechsler Pre-School and Primary Scale of Intelligence (WPPSI)

PERSONALITY AND INTEREST TESTS

California Psychological Inventory (CPI)
Drawing Tests
House-Tree-Person Projective Technique (H-T-P)
Kuder Interest Inventories
Minnesota Counseling Inventory
Minnesota Multiphasic Personality Inventory (MMPI)
Rorschach
Strong-Campbell Interest Inventory (SCII)
Thematic Apperception Test (TAT)

SPECIAL DIAGNOSTIC TESTS

Bender-Gestalt
The Culture Fair Intelligence Test
Tests for the Blind
Tests for the Hearing Handicapped
Tests for the Orthopedic Handicapped

ACHIEVEMENT AND APTITUDE TESTS, INCLUDING INTELLIGENCE TESTS

General Aptitude Test Battery

The U.S. Employment Service produced the *General Apti-*

tude Test Battery (GATB), which is used throughout the country to help guide people seeking work. The battery is given by state employment services and other nonprofit agencies whose personnel have been trained in the use of the test by the Employment Service. High school juniors and seniors often take the GATB through a cooperative plan that makes the results available to high school counselors and the Employment Service. Versions of the test have been prepared for a number of foreign countries.

The test was constructed to help guide persons into suitable work. Each of the thousands of jobs in the modern industrial world has its own aptitude requirements. When an employer asks for referrals of potential employees, he or she wants applicants likely to succeed. Thus, the U.S. Employment Service, working with state agencies, conducts studies of the psychological characteristics of particular jobs and accumulates information on the implications of a test score. The following illustrates some of the occupations surveyed: assembler of dry-cell batteries, aircraft electrician, teacher, x-ray technician, nurse's aide, sheet-metal worker, baker, cook, spot welder, comptometer operator, corn-husking-machine operator, knitting-machine fixer, food packer.

Predictions for such jobs take us far beyond the academic and reasoning ability required by most aptitude tests. The diversity of occupations rules out the possibility of devising a separate aptitude test for each job. For guidance, a limited number of diversified tests are needed that everyone can take and that can be linked together in various combinations to predict success in different situations. With this end in view, the current GATB measures nine distinctive factors:

G — General reasoning ability (a composite of tests entitled Vocabulary, Three-Dimensional Space, and Arithmetic Reasoning)
V — Verbal aptitude (Vocabulary)
N — Numerical aptitude (Computation, Arithmetic, Reasoning)
S — Spatial aptitude (Three-Dimensional Space)
P — Form perception (Tool Matching, Form Matching)

Q — Clerical perception (Name Comparison)
K — Motor coordination (Mark Making)
F — Finger dexterity (Assemble, Disassemble)
M — Manual dexterity (Place, Turn)

No similar test exceeds the efficiency of the GATB. Each of its paper-and-pencil tests takes about six minutes. The psychomotor tests require even less working time, but several minutes are used for demonstration practice. The entire battery can be given in two and one-quarter hours. The simple procedures allow trustworthy administration of the tests by relatively untrained examiners to subjects who have limited education or poor command of English. The psychomotor tests are designed so that each subject leaves all the materials as they were found — ready for the next subject.

This marked speeding of nearly all the GATB subtests may reduce their validity for many purposes, especially if the person has some reading deficit, is upset by tests, or has taken few tests. But since the U.S. Employment Service has access to workers in all areas of the country, all types of industry and agriculture, and most occupational levels, a highly representative normal sample was used. Four thousand cases were selected from the records on hand to form a group that was representative of all occupational, sex, and age groups in proportion to census data.

Test results are reported as standard scores with a mean of 100 and a standard deviation of 20. Extensive research has demonstrated good reliability and validity, but the latter does vary between and among different occupations. The social service practitioner should use the GATB in conjunction with the U.S. Employment Service's *Dictionary of Occupations*.

Goodenough-Harris Drawing Test

The *Goodenough-Harris Drawing Test (Draw-A-Man Test)* was designed for children five to fifteen years of age to evaluate intelligence by analysis of the child's drawings of a man and a woman. It can be used as an initial screening test, a rapid way of gaining an impression of a child's general ability levels, and a means of estimating the mental ability of children for whom the usual verbal tests of ability are inappropriate.

The test booklets provide three spaces for the child to produce drawings of a man, a woman, and a self-portrait. The examiner asks the child to draw the best picture possible and cautions him to make a whole person, not simply a head-and-shoulders view. Although there are no time limits on the test, the child usually completes it in ten to fifteen minutes. Tests may be administered to groups or individuals.

The test contains fairly explicit scoring directions. According to research, it has relatively high coefficients of interscorer reliability (approximately .90), but tests for test-retest reliability range only from a high of .94 for a one-day interval to .65 for a three-year interval between testings.

The Draw-A-Man Test's validity has been assessed primarily by correlations with scores on other tests. Correlations with the earlier forms of the Stanford-Binet range from .30 to .74; reports show correlations of this test and the WISC between .40 and .50.

Samples of 300 children at each age level from five to fifteen years, selected as representative of the population of the United States according to father's occupation and geographic region, established norms for these scoring scales. (The test manual reports standard score norms that have a mean of 100 and a standard deviation of 15.)

Because the standardized sample varied only in regard to a few critical variables (such as father's occupation and geographic region), the norms may not be useful for special ethnic groups such as American Indians or residents of remote rural areas. Also, this test's validity has been investigated primarily by comparison with scores on other tests.

Thus, the Draw-A-Man Test may only indicate generally the likelihood of a child scoring well on another test and may be invalid as a predictor of potential performance in training programs. The social service practitioner should regard this test with caution, for it only roughly estimates intellectual ability. It should be supplemented with other measures of general intellectual ability.

Otis Self-Administering Test of Mental Ability

An early test that has been used widely in personnel screening on a group basis is the *Otis Self-Administering Test of Mental Ability*. This test also helped to develop the basis for the highest level norms for *Otis Quick-Scoring Mental Ability Tests* used as an academic screening device from the early grades through high school level. Industry uses the Otis Self-Administering Test of Mental Ability to screen applicants for varied jobs such as clerk, calculating machine operator, assembly line worker, and foreman and other supervisory personnel. A number of validation studies have correlated the Otis with an industrial criterion, and most have demonstrated that the applicants' scores compare with actual job performance, yielding highly significant validity coefficients. In semiskilled jobs, the Otis Test correlates moderately well with success in learning the job and ease of initial adaptation. But it does not correlate highly with subsequent job achievement. This would be expected for routine jobs but also holds true for high-level, professional jobs, since it discriminates poorly at upper levels.

Peabody Picture Vocabulary Test

The *Peabody Picture Vocabulary Test*, designed to provide a verbal intelligence estimate through measuring recognition vocabulary, is effective with average subjects and has special value with certain other groups. Because reading is not required, the scale is especially fair for nonreaders, and since responses are non-oral, the test can be used for the speech impaired (expressly the aphasiac and the stutterer). Also, it is used with certain autistic, withdrawn, and psychotic persons. The test can be used with orthopedically handicapped and cerebral-palsied persons and with some visually handicapped and perceptually impaired persons. Thus, the scale allows for any English-speaking resident of the United States between two years, six months and eighteen years who can hear words, see the drawings, and indicate "yes" or "no" in a manner that communicates. The *Peabody Picture Vocabulary Test* has a number of advantages:

1. The test has high interest value and thus establishes good rapport.
2. It needs no extensive, specialized preparation for its administration.
3. It is given in ten to fifteen minutes.
4. Scoring is objective and completed within one to two minutes.
5. It is untimed; thus, it is a power rather than a speed test.
6. No oral response is required.
7. Alternative forms of the test are provided.

The administration of the Peabody Picture Vocabulary Test requires no special preparation other than complete familiarity with the test procedure, which includes administering it prior to its use as a standardized measure. The examiner must know the correct pronunciation of each of the test words as given in *Webster's New Collegiate Dictionary.* If all the instructions are observed, psychologists, teachers, speech therapists, physicians, counselors, and social workers should be able to give the scale accurately.

Ten to fifteen minutes usually are required for this untimed test. The scale is administered only over the critical range of items for a particular subject. The starting point, basal, and ceiling vary from testee to testee. The examiner presents a series of pictures to each subject. There are four pictures to a page, and each is numbered. The examiner states a word describing one of the pictures and asks the subject to point to or tell the number of the picture that the word describes.

By using special tables, the raw score can be converted to three types of derived scores:

1. Age equivalent (mental age)
2. Standard-score equivalent (intelligence quotient)
3. Percentile equivalent

The age norms for converting raw scores to mental-age scores on the Peabody Picture Vocabulary Test are given in the manual. Age equivalents supposedly provide an index of the level of a given subject's development. For example, 75 is the mean raw score on Form A for children who have a chronological age of 10.0. Therefore, regardless of subjects' chronological ages, if they obtain a raw score of 75 on a Peabody Picture Vocabulary Test, they purportedly possess a mental age of 10.0 years, since their ability to score on this test is like that of the average ten-year-old. Approximate grade equivalents derive from age equivalents by the standard of five; that is, a child with a mental age of 11.0 would have a grade equivalent of six (subtract five from the mental age), indicating an accumulative capacity to achieve at the beginning grade six level. (Age norms have a number of advantages: They provide an easily understood index of the subject's developmental level; are useful in comparing mental age with chronological age, achievement age, social age, and so on; and provide standard-score norms that may offer an "index of brightness" for a given child in comparison with other children of the same age.) The Peabody was standardized with a mean of 100 and a standard deviation of 15.

Stanford-Binet Scale

The *Stanford-Binet Scale* for measuring intelligence has undergone two revisions since 1937 (1960 and 1972), each using a common principle: The average capacities of children of various ages represent differences in degrees of brightness along with differences in levels of development. With each revision has come better normative data and increased reliability. Although it is acknowledged to be a verbally saturated test (particularly at higher levels), it continues to be the test of choice for normal children up to the age of eight years and for retarded children and adults.

The following procedure describes the method of scoring the Stanford-Binet Scale. The examiner selects a starting point in a range of tasks where the subject can pass all items. This is called the basal year. The examiner then proceeds upward in the scale until the subject fails all items, a level called the ceiling year. Each item carries specified credit in terms of months contributing to a mental-age score. These credits, added to the age value of the basal year, yield the mental-age score. For example, assume a subject has a basal year of six; three test items are passed at the seven-year level, giving an additional credit of six months; two are passed at the eight-year level, giving further credit for four months; but all are failed at the nine-year level (ceiling year). Thus, the subject's mental age is six years, ten months.

Performance materials included in the test demand that the subject do something — build a pattern, make a design with blocks, or fill in a form built with variously shaped blocks. Other nonverbal materials include such activities as copying a geometric figure, completing the picture of a man, and discriminating between forms. In all these instances the child must use verbal ability, since he must understand verbal directions. Moreover, verbal ability also can be a factor if the child's knowledge of the names of the objects or geometric figures helps the manipulation of classification. In short, the Stanford-Binet Scale is a verbally saturated test.

Vineland Social Maturity Scale

The *Vineland Social Maturity Scale,* designed for use with individuals from infancy to the age of thirty years, models itself on the construction and standardization of the Stanford-Binet Scale.

Unlike many other scales, this scale is based on a well-defined rationale and systematic construction. It groups behavior items at age levels as in the Stanford-Binet; these items represent progressive maturation and adjustment to the environment in the following categories:

1. Self-help — reaches for nearby objects (age 0-1).
2. Self-direction — buys own clothing (15-18).
3. Locomotion — walks about room unattended (age 1-2).
4. Occupation — helps at little household tasks (age 3-4); systematizes own work (age 25 plus).
5. Communication — makes telephone calls (age 10-11).

6. Socialization — demands personal attention (age 0-1); advances general welfare (age 25 plus).

Examiners score items after interviewing the subject or another person well acquainted with the subject. A social age then is obtained and is divided by chronological age, yielding a social quotient (S.Q.).

Although this social maturity scale correlates highly with intelligence test results (about .80), the author of the Vineland Scale maintains that its content and rated functions are distinct enough for use in the study of an individual's general behavioral development, since social age provides a procedural basis to guide the care and training of an individual.

While the scale aids in diagnosing a normal population as well as the mentally deficient, it was conceived to facilitate the diagnosis of mental retardation. Primarily, it differentiates between mentally retarded individuals who can conduct their personal and social lives with a degree of independence and the mentally retarded who are socially inadequate.

There is widespread clinical use of the Vineland Scale with children and adolescents. In addition, it is a valuable device for interviewing and counseling parents and children.

Wechsler Adult Intelligence Scale

The *Wechsler Adult Intelligence Scale (WAIS)* is used to assess general and specific intellectual ability of persons sixteen years and above. The WAIS consists of eleven subtests grouped into a Verbal scale and a Performance scale.

VERBAL SCALE

1. *Information:* Includes twenty-nine questions covering a wide variety of information that adults in our culture presumably should acquire. An effort was made to avoid specialized or academic knowledge.
2. *Comprehension:* Includes fourteen items requiring the subject to explain what should be done under certain circumstances, why certain practices are followed, the meaning of proverbs, etc. The items are designed to mea-

sure practical judgment and common sense. This test resembles comprehension items on the Stanford-Binet, but its specific content was chosen to be more consonant with the interests and activities of adults.

3. *Arithmetic:* Includes fourteen problems similar to those encountered in elementary school arithmetic. Each problem, orally presented, is to be solved without the use of paper and pencil.

4. *Similarities:* Includes fifteen items requiring the subject to say how two things are alike.

5. *Digit Span:* Includes orally presented lists of three to nine digits to be reproduced orally. In the second part, the subject must reproduce backwards lists of two to eight digits.

6. *Vocabulary:* Includes forty words of increasing difficulty presented both orally and visually. The subject is asked what each word means.

PERFORMANCE SCALE

7. *Digit Symbol:* This is a version of a familiar code-substitution test that dates to the early *Woodworth-Wells Association Test* and often has been included in nonlanguage intelligence scales. The key contains nine symbols paired with nine digits. The subject's score is the number of symbols correctly written within one and one-half minutes.

8. *Picture Completion:* Includes twenty-one cards, each containing a picture with some part missing. The subject must tell what is missing from each picture.

9. *Block Design:* This test consists of increasingly complex designs made from four to nine cubes. The cubes or blocks have red, white, and red-and-white sides.

10. *Picture Arrangement:* Each item consists of a set of cards containing pictures to be rearranged in proper sequence to tell a story.

11. *Object Assembly:* Includes a number of pieces to be assembled much in the manner of a jigsaw puzzle. The

subtest includes four pictures to be reproduced, including those of a mannequin, hand, profile of a face, and side view of an elephant.

Speech and accuracy of performance are taken into account in scoring Arithmetic, Digit Symbol, Block Design, Picture Arrangement, and Object Assembly Tests.

The WAIS standardization sample was chosen carefully to ensure representativeness. The principal normative sample consisted of 1,700 cases, including an equal number of men and women distributed over seven age levels between sixteen and sixty-four years. Subjects were selected to match as closely as possible the proportions of the 1950 U.S. Census with regard to geographic residence, urban-rural residence, race, white versus nonwhite, occupational level, and education. One man and one woman from an institution for mental defectives were included for each age level. Supplementary norms for older persons were established by testing an "old-age sample" of 475 persons aged sixty years and over in a typical Midwestern city.

Raw scores on each WAIS subtest are converted to standard scores with a mean of 10 and a standard deviation of 3. These scaled scores were derived from a reference group of 500 cases that included all persons between the ages of twenty and thirty-four in the standardization sample. All subtest scores are expressed in comparable units. Verbal, Performance, and Full Scale scores are found by adding the scaled scores on the six Verbal subtests, the five Performance subtests, and all eleven subtests, respectively. The manual provides tables that convert these three scores to deviation I.Q.s with a mean of 100 and a standard deviation of 15. However, such I.Q.s are found according to the specific age group. Thus, they show an individual's standing in comparison with persons of his or her own age level. Deriving I.Q.s separately for each age level compares the individuals with the declining norm beyond the peak age. The age decrement is greater in Performance than Verbal scores and varies from one subtest to another. Thus, Digit Symbol, with its heavy dependence on speed and visual perception, shows the maximum age decline. However, on the other Performance subtests, speed may be an unimportant factor in the observed decline. In a special study of this point, subjects in the old-age sample were given those tests under both timed and untimed conditions. Not only were the score differences under the two conditions slight, but the decrements from the 60-64 to 70-74 age group virtually were the same under timed and untimed conditions.

The WAIS has demonstrated consistently high reliability coefficients through the split-half reliability technique. Validity has been investigated primarily through correlations between test scores and scholastic achievement. The WAIS also has been compared with other instruments for similarity in scores achieved by the same subjects. In all respects the WAIS has demonstrated relatively high correlations. In summary, then, *the WAIS perhaps is the best general adult intelligance test available.*

Wechsler Intelligence Scale for Children

Examiners frequently use the *Wechsler Intelligence Scale for Children (WISC* — an individually administered general-intelligence test — to predict academic success or discover intellectual or academic deficiencies that may be interfering with school achievement. Like the Wechsler Adult Intelligence Scale, the WISC obtains I.Q.s by comparing each subject's test performance with the scores earned by individuals in his or her age group. An I.Q. score obtained by subsequent WISC retest always compares the subject with his or her age group at each time of testing. Each person tested is assigned an I.Q. that represents the intelligence rating relative to his or her age. The WISC uses a mean of 100 and a standard deviation of 15 and places I.Q.s from 90 to 110 in the average range. In terms of percentile limits, the highest one percent would have I.Q.s of 135 and above and the lowest one percent of I.Q.s to 65 and below. The middle 50 percent of children in each age will have I.Q.s ranging from 90 to 110.

Like the adult scales, the WISC consists of twelve subtests that are divided into two subgroups identified as Verbal and Performance. The Verbal subtests are Information, Comprehension, Arithmetic, Similarities, Vocabulary, and Digit Span; the Performance subtests are Picture Completion, Picture Arrangement, Block Design, Object Assembling, Coding, and Mazes.

In the standardization of the WISC, every subject took all twelve tests, but to shorten the time required for examination the scale has been reduced to ten tests. (The Digit Span in the Verbal and Mazes in the Performance part were omitted primarily on the basis of their relatively low correlation with the other tests on the scale and, in the case of Mazes, the time factor.) One can use all subtests, but in this case all twelve tests must be prorated before computing the I.Q.s. A trained clinical or school psychologist usually administers the test.

Wechsler Pre-School and Primary Scale of Intelligence

Published in 1967, the *Wechsler Pre-School and Primary Scale of Intelligence (WPPSI)* is designed to test the intelligence of children from ages four to six and one-half years. The scale includes eleven subtests, ten of which determine the I.Q. score. Eight of the subtests are downward extensions and adaptations of the Wechsler Intelligence Scale for Children. The other three replace WISC subtests that proved unsuitable.

As in the WISC and WAIS, the subtests group into Verbal and Performance scales from which Verbal, Performance, and Full Scale I.Q.s are found. To enhance variety and help maintain the young child's interest and cooperation, the administration of Verbal and Performance subtests is alternated in the WPPSI. Total testing time ranges from fifty to seventy-five minutes in one or two testing sessions. Abbreviated scales or short forms of the scale are not recommended.

The subtests of the WPPSI include Information, Vocabulary, Arithmetic, Similarities, Comprehension, Sentences, Animal House, Picture Completion, Mazes, Geometric Design, and Block Design. Sentences is a memory test substituted for the WISC Digit Span. The child repeats each sentence immediately after the examiner presents it orally. This test can be alternately used for one of the other Verbal tests if it is administered as an additional test to seek further information about the child; it is not included in the total score for calculating the I.Q. Animal House similar basically to the WAIS Digit Symbol and the WISC coding test. A key at the top of the board has pictures of a dog, chicken, fish, and cat, each with a differently colored cylinder (its "house") under it. The child should insert the correctly colored cylinder in the hole beneath each animal on the board. Time, errors, and omissions determine the score. Geometric Design requires the copying of ten simple designs with a colored pencil.

The WPPSI was standardized on a national sample of 1,200 boys and girls. The sample was stratified against 1960 census data with reference to geographical region, urban-rural residence, proportion of whites and nonwhites, and father's occupational level. Raw scores on each subtest are converted to normalized standard scores with a mean of 10 and a standard deviation of 3 within each one-fourth-year group. The sum of the scaled scores on the Verbal, Performance, and Full Scale are converted to deviation I.Q.s with a mean of 100 and a standard deviation of 15. Although Wechsler advised against using mental-age scores because of their possible misinterpretation, the manual provides a table for converting subtest raw scores to "test ages" in one-fourth-year units.

Reliability coefficients for the Full Scale I.Q. are acceptably high and consistent with the other Wechsler scales. The manual provides tables for evaluating the significance of score differences. These data suggest that a difference of fifteen points or more between the Verbal and Performance I.Q. is significant enough to be investigated. Stability over time also was checked in a group of fifty kindergarten children retested after an average interval of eleven weeks. Under these conditions, the reliability coefficients for the Full Scale I.Q., Verbal I.Q., and Performance I.Q. were satisfactorily high.

The procedures followed in standardizing the scale and estimating reliability and validity are of uniformly high technical quality. The size and the composition of the norm and sample are advanced considerably over the pre-school tests previously available. But observe caution when using any test score involving young children; many variables, difficult to control, affect the uncertain procedure of assessing young children.

PERSONALITY AND INTEREST TESTS

California Psychological Inventory

The *California Psychological Inventory (CPI)* is one of the few self-report personality inventories not based on a pathological model of personality, i.e. it purports to measure normal personality functioning. Used for clients thirteen years and older, the CPI contains 480 true/false items, can be given to individuals or groups, and takes from forty-five minutes to one hour to administer.

About half the items in the CPI were taken from the Minnesota Multiphasic Personality Inventory (to be discussed). The test yields eighteen scales that are divided into four classes of behavior. The classes of behavior, scales in each class, and scale abbreviations are presented as follows:

Class I —measure of poise, ascendancy, and self-assurance; contains scales indicating Dominance (*Do*), Capacity for Status (*Cs*), Sociability (*Sy*), Social Presence (*Sp*), Self-Acceptance (*Sa*), and Well-Being (*Wb*).

Class II —measures of socialization, maturity, and social responsibility; contains scales indicating Responsibility (*Re*), Socialization (*So*), Self-Control (*Sc*), Tolerance (*To*), Good Impression (*Gi*), and Communality (*Cm*).

Class III—measures of achievement potential and intellectual efficiency; contains scales indicating Achievement via Conformance (*Ac*), Achievement via Independence (*Ai*), and Intellectual Efficiency (*Ie*).

Class IV—measures of personal orientation and attitudes toward life; contains scales indicating Psychological-Mindedness (*Py*), Flexibility (*Fx*), and Femininity (*Fe*).

Scores for each scale are reported in standard-score form with a mean of 50 and standard deviation of 10. Test norms from a large general sample are provided along with norms for many special groups. According to its constructor (Gough), each scale on the CPI is designed to predict what an individual will do in a specific context and/or identify individuals who will be described in a certain way.

After twenty years of evaluative research, the CPI ranks among the best of the personality measures. Furthermore, it has some of the highest validity coefficients yet reports in terms of predicting criteria such as success in foster parenting, supervisor ratings of police performance, and success in student teaching.

In general, the CPI should be interpreted clinically on the total configuration, or combinations, or all eighteen scales, and not on one scale alone. The use of the CPI requires a professionally trained, experienced practitioner.

Other Drawing Tests

Although almost every art medium, technique, and type of subject matter has been investigated in the search for significant diagnostic clues, special attention centers on drawings of the human figure. The *Machover Draw-A-Person Test* is a well-known example. In this test, the examiner provides the subject with a letter-size sheet of paper and a medium-soft pencil and tells him/her to simply "draw a person" or — to young children — "draw somebody" or "draw a boy or girl." On completion of the first drawing, the examiner asks the subject to draw a person of the opposite sex from the first figure. While the subject draws, the examiner notes comments, the sequence in which parts are drawn, and other procedural details. An inquiry may follow this drawing in which the subject is asked to make up a story about each person drawn "as if he were a character in a play or novel." During the inquiry a series of questions elicits specific information about age, schooling, occupation, family, and other facts associated with the characters portrayed.

Qualitative judgments, involving the preparation of a composite personality description from the analysis of the many features of the drawing, are made in the evaluation of the human figure. For example, each major body part, such as head, individual facial features, hair, neck, shoulders, breast, trunk, hips, and extremities, is regarded as significant in the scoring criteria.

The interpretive guide to the Machover Draw-A-Person Test contains sweeping generalizations such as "disproportionately large heads often will be given by individuals suffering from organic brain disease," or "the sex given the proportionately larger head is the sex that is accorded more intellectual and social authority." But research evidence does not support these speculations. The manual also refers to a "file of thousands of drawings" examined in clinical context and includes a few selected clinical cases for illustrative purposes, but no systematic presentation of data accompanies the published test reports.

Validation studies of this test by other investigators have yielded conflicting results. Attempts to develop semi-objective scoring procedures that use rating scales or checklists have met with little success. The test may prove to be more valuable for use with children and other relatively naive subjects than for sophisticated adult groups. Although it appears to differentiate seriously disturbed persons from normals, its discriminative value within relatively normal groups is questionable.

House-Tree-Person Projective Technique

The *House-Tree-Person Projective Technique (H-T-P)*, devised by Buck, has aroused considerable interest as witnessed by the number of relevant research publications. In this test, the subject is told to draw as well as possible a picture of a house, a tree, and a person. Meanwhile, the examiner takes copious notes on time, sequence of parts drawn, spontaneous comments by the subject, and expressions of emotion. Oral inquiry, including a long set of standardized questions, follows completion of the drawing. The examiner analyzes the drawings both quantitatively and qualitatively, chiefly on the basis of their formal or stylistic characteristics.

In discussing the rationale underlying the choice of objects to draw, Buck maintains the "house" should arouse association concerning the subject's home and those persons with whom he/she lives; "tree" should evoke associations pertaining to life goals and ability to derive satisfaction from the environment in general; "person" should evoke associations involving interpersonal relationships. Some clinicians may find helpful leads in such drawings when considered jointly with other information about the individual case. The elaborate, lengthy administrative and scoring procedures described by Buck appear unwarranted in light of the highly inadequate nature of the supporting data.

Kuder Interest Inventories

Kuder Inventories, which measure interests for different purposes or in different ways, employ items in each inventory consisting of three activities. The test taker must choose the activity he/she likes the most and least for each item.

The *Kuder Vocational Preference Record (KVPR)* provides scores on ten interest areas and a verification scale used to detect inconsistencies or unlikely answers. The interest areas are outdoor, mechanical, computational, scientific, persuasive, artistic, literary, musical, social service, and clerical. A list of occupations grouped according to major interest area or pair of interest areas is provided in the test manual. Norms for high school and college students and for adults are provided for both sexes. Scores are reported in percentiles.

Reliability of the KVPR is fairly high (around .90), and validity has been established. The validation research has been conducted mainly against a criterion of job satisfaction.

The *Kuder Occupational Interest Survey (KOIS)* provides twenty-nine occupational and nineteen college-major interest scales for females and seventy-seven occupational and twenty-nine college-major interest scales for males. Scale scores on the KOIS indicate how highly the examinee's responses correlate with interest patterns of specific occupational groups. The closer the correspondence between an individual's responses and persons in the occupational group, the higher the individual's interest in that occupation. Major validation work on the KOIS has not been reported.

The *Kuder General Interest Survey (KGIS)* is based on the KVPR and was developed for grades six through twelve. The scores are reported in percentiles for both tests. Norms are reported for a limited adult sample and a large national stratified sample for boys and girls.

Minnesota Counseling Inventory

An effort to adapt the previously discussed Minnesota Multiphasic Personality Inventory for use with normal high school students and college freshmen led to the development of the *Minnesota Counseling Inventory.* Many of the 355 true/false items of the latter inventory came from the MMPI, and several other scales bear a close resemblance to the MMPI scales.

With norms based on more than 20,000 high school students tested in ten states, the Minnesota Counseling Inventory provides scores in seven areas designated as Family Relationships, Social Relationships, Emotional Stability, Conformity, Adjustment to Reality, Mood, and Leadership. The Conformity scale has a strong resemblance to the MMPI Pd scale, and Adjustment to Reality similarly resembles the Sc scale. Also, two verification scores exhibit similar traits to the MMPI validity scales. The comparison of random samples of students with groups nominated by teachers as outstanding examples of the quality tests validated the total scores on the different scales. Test reliability established by split-half and retest procedures is at an acceptable level. The seven area scores, however, are not as distinct as their titles imply. Only counselors familiar enough with its construction to evaluate its complex scores should use this inventory.

Minnesota Multiphasic Personality Inventory

The design of the *Minnesota Multiphasic Personality Inven-*

tory (MMPI) provides an objective assessment of some of the major personality characteristics that affect personal and social adjustment. The scales provide a measurement of the personality traits of literate adolescents and adults, together with standards for evaluating the acceptability and dependability of each test record. Nine scales were developed originally for the test's clinical use and were named for the abnormal conditions on which their construction was based. Since they have proved meaningful within the normal range of behavior, these scales now are referred to by their abbreviations — Hs (hypochondriasis), D (depression), Hy (hysteria), Pd (psychopathic deviate), Mf (masculinity-femininity), Pa (paranoia), Pt (psychoasthenia), Sc (schizophrenia), and Ma (hypomania) — to avoid possible misleading connotations. Development of these test items has produced a number of other scales: Si (social introversion) commonly is scored, as well as three validating scales, L (lie), F (validity), and K (correction). Untrained personnel can administer this inventory; however, a thoroughly trained clinical or counseling psychologist should interpret the results.

One can expect test subjects sixteen years or older with at least six years of successful schooling to complete the MMPI without difficulty. When an individual is specifically referred for testing, one generally can ascertain beforehand whether the MMPI is appropriate for use, thereby avoiding embarrassment that would arise from failure during the actual administration. The full-scale edition of the MMPI requires the subject to give a true/false response to 550 questions (*see* Table I). The raw scores are converted to a standardized score called a *T* score (*see* Table I) on which the MMPI profile and code are based. The test items are presented in card form for individual use or in a booklet with a separate answer sheet for individual examination or large-scale group-testing programs. This yields a profile for the clinical comparison of the relative strengths and weaknesses of the characteristics purportedly measured.

The MMPI should not be evaluated on the basis of one scale alone but rather on the pattern of scores for the entire nine scales, including the validity indicators. For example, a high score on the schizophrenia scale does not necessarily indicate the presence or absence of schizophrenia. The test affords a vast number of patterns. Thus, although scorers might think that they have seen a pattern several times, the possibility of encountering duplicate patterns is slight.

The MMPI was thought of originally as an aid to psychiatric diagnosis and evaluation, but it has been used in many different settings and validated against hundreds of criteria. The rapid rise of the nonpsychiatric application of the MMPI has stimulated substantial growth in new scales and scoring procedures.

Reliability and validity research results on the MMPI are not entirely convincing. The test/retest reliability coefficients range from .46 to .93, with the majority lying between MMPI profile scores and actual psychiatric diagnoses, even though the instrument was developed initially for this purpose. In approximately 60 percent of the cases, diagnoses from the MMPI correctly predicted corresponding clinical diagnoses.

Indeed, the available categories of psychiatric diagnoses are subject to criticism, since it is questionable whether or not the MMPI actually achieves its intended objectives when used only in clinical situations. Where the MMPI is used to screen large populations such as military recruits, college students, or business executives, it serves as a reasonably general screening device. It is most helpful in identifying persons who achieve extreme scores on the subscales and thus require further study.

The use of the MMPI requires professionally trained, experienced, and sophisticated practitioners because of the complexity of the personality characteristics of the inventory, the meanings of the scales, and the way in which the scales relate to each other in predicting behavior.

The original MMPI was standardized on a sample of about 700 normal visitors (ranging in age from sixteen to fifty-five and representing a cross section of the Minnesota population) at the University of Minnesota Hospital, in contrast to some 800 clinical cases (from the Neuro-Psychiatric Division of the University of Minnesota Hospital).

Rorschach

The *Rorschach,* or "inkblot" test, developed in 1921 by Hermann Rorschach, is used primarily as a personality test based on the "projective" method. The test consists of ten inkblots presented one at a time to the subject. Five of the first seven blots are black and white, but blots two and three have smaller red blotches. The last three blots are multicolored. Typically, the test is administered individually in three phases. During the first phase, the subject gives spontaneous responses to the inkblots. During the second, or "inquiry," phase, the examiner asks questions to determine how the "characteristics" of the inkblots triggered the subject's response, e.g. did color, shape, or shading help the person identify what he or she saw? In a later phase occasionally used called "testing the limits," the examiner attempts to gather additional scoring material, especially if the subject has given unusual responses or has not seen the concepts commonly seen.

The Rorschach scoring system allots five scores to a response. The scoring is determined according to the area chosen, the content chosen, the form level of the response (how accurately or arbitrarily or how definitely or vaguely the response form is conceived), and the popularity of the response (whether or not the response is found frequently or rarely).

In addition to the Rorschach's complex scoring, a qualitative approach also can provide further data. The way a subject approaches the card, the pauses, the difficulties, the apparently extraneous comments — all can offer further data when interpreted by a skilled clinician.

Although the Rorschach has been used for more than fifty years, and extensive research has been conducted to establish its predictive validity, the results have proven somewhat disappointing and uneven. In research experiments, clinicians who were asked to make a diagnosis based on Rorschach responses alone, without any other data available, could not accurately predict behavior or diagnose psychiatric disorders. The research indicates that the Rorschach is inconstant; sometimes it works while other times it does not. In general, most clinicians agree that the Rorschach has some predictive validity that does better than chance alone. But experienced examiners do equally well by asking subjects direct questions. However, apparently no empirical evidence demonstrates that the Rorschach or any other projective instrument will predict behavior reliably in the day-to-day world. As a tool for making decisions regarding practical problems, therefore, the instrument is limited.

A number of split-half and test/retest reliability studies are available on Rorschach protocols. Reported values differ considerably from study to study and for different types of subscores. However, in general, the use of a specific scoring system produces uniformly positive and fairly high correlations in many cases.

The Rorschach, like other projective tests, is a clinical instrument that should give reliable, valid results only when used by persons having special technical training and sophistication in understanding and applying specific personality theory. The tests generally are time consuming to give and to score, and they sometimes are difficult to justify, considering the results obtained. It is the authors' impression that a highly experienced clinician, willing to engage the subject in in-depth interviews, can obtain similar results and perhaps make more meaningful inferences regarding behavior prediction.

Strong-Campbell Interest Inventory

One of the most widely used interest tests is the *Strong-Campbell Interest Inventory (SCII)*, which is a major revision of the Strong Vocational Interest Blank first published in 1927. The 1974 revision contains 325 items divided into seven parts. Items in the first five sections require a "like-indifferent-dislike" response to activities or topics such as biology, fishing, being an aviator, planning a sales campaign, etc. The remaining two parts require the examinee to choose a preference between paired items and make a set of self-descriptive statements, i.e. "yes," "no," or "?".

The results of the SCII are reported in twenty-three Basic

Interest Scales divided into six General Occupational Themes. The General Occupational Themes are realistic, investigative, artistic, social, enterprising, and general. Interest scores on General Occupational Themes are reported in the form of standard scores based on the distribution of the whole norm group. All standard scores reported on all phases of the tests have a mean of 50 and a standard deviation of 10. Interpretive phases, e.g. high, very low, based on the same-sex subgroup also are reported.

The Basic Interest Scales, included in General Occupational Themes, further limit the areas of interest. For example, Basic Interest areas of music, dramatics, art, and writing are contained in the Artistic General Occupational Theme. Standard scores again are based on the whole norm group, while profiles are plotted against the same-sex subgroup.

The SCII provides a profile with standard scores on 124 occupational scales, e.g. police officer, psychologist. Standard scores are reported for male and female subgroups (when available), while profiles are plotted against the same-sex subgroup.

The SCII also includes an Administrative Index (used to detect invalid tests) and scales indicating Academic Orientation (the tendency to continue one's education) and Introversion-Extroversion.

The normative group for the General Occupation Themes and Basic Interest Scales of the SCII comprised 300 men and 300 women representative of all occupations contained in the inventory. Items for the Occupational Scales were selected by comparing responses of the criterion group, such as police officers, to a reference group. A weighted scoring system is used to assess how closely an examinee's interests correspond to those of the reference group. For example, if an examinee's responses correspond closely to a reference group, e.g. police officer, his/her interest in that occupation would be rated high.

Extensive research has demonstrated a high degree of reliability and validity for the SCII. Several studies have measured predictive validity over long periods. Results indicate substantial correspondence between initial occupational profiles and occupations generally pursued. Finally, it should be noted that the complexity of the SCII requires computer scoring.

Thematic Apperception Test

The *Thematic Apperception Test,* a projective personality test commonly referred to as the *TAT,* consists of thirty picture cards and one blank card. An examiner uses the cards in various combinations, depending on sex and age; some are used with all subjects and others with only one sex or age group. With any subject the examiner uses only twenty total pictures that usually are administered in two test sessions, ten pictures at a time.

Examinees are told that the TAT tests imagination. They are asked to make up stories to suit themselves and are assured that no right or wrong responses exist. The examiner shows pictures one at a time, simply instructing the subject to respond as follows:

1. Tell what he/she thinks led to the depicted scene: how it came about.
2. Give an account of what is happening and the feelings of the characters in the picture.
3. Predict the outcome.

There are no time limits; in fact, the examiner encourages the subject to work with a picture for as long as five minutes. Sometimes the examiner uses an interview to investigate the origins of the stories, expecially associations as to places, names of persons, dates, etc. This is an important aspect of the process, because it enables the examiner to clarify the stories' meanings. For instance, a boy ten years of age created a surprising number of stories dealing with death. The interview revealed that these were normal responses: The boy's father was an undertaker, and they lived near the funeral parlor.

Although the TAT pictures are more structured than an inkblot, they are ambiguous enough to allow wide latitude for individual differences in responses. The TAT, like the Rorschach, is a projective method. Murray designed the TAT to evaluate "drives, sentiments, and conflicts" by analyzing the story produced by the subject. He based the test on the principle that when interpreting an ambiguous social situation, one is apt to unconsciously reveal aspects of one's own personality that would not or could not be admitted otherwise. While absorbing the picture and attempting to construct an appropriate account of it, the subject is off guard and becomes increasingly unaware of himself/herself. In creating stories based on vague pictures, the subject uses information stemming from unique personal experiences. The examiner regards everything the subject says as having meaning. From these stories, the skilled examiner/interpreter draws inferences regarding the subject's personality traits and their organization.

The limitations of other projective devices apply to the TAT. Several elaborate and special purpose schemes allow scoring of the TAT, but they show little procedural uniformity for analyzing test results, and few clinicians report the specific system in use. Thus, comparisons between examiners often are impossible.

Unless one of two objective scoring systems is used by a trainer scorer, reliability for the TAT generally is low.

Validity research has not demonstrated the TAT's practical use. It has limited capacity to predict behavior and thus is of little value in decision making. It has been useful, however, for research in achievement motivation.

SPECIAL DIAGNOSTIC TESTS

A variety of tests have been developed for a number of specialized purposes. The following are examples of special purpose tests with references to further information for the consumer.

Bender-Gestalt

The *Bender-Gestalt* was designed to test visual-motor performance skills. It is used as an aid in assessing perceptual-motor coordination disorders that may be related to organic brain dysfunction. The test also has proven somewhat useful in diagnosing various types of retardation and personality functioning.

The Bender-Gestalt consists of nine geometric figures printed on cards. The subject is asked to reproduce the figures. This basic procedure, called the copy phase, is in some adaptations of the Bender-Gestalt. For example, the examiner may ask subjects to recall, elaborate on, or change the figures they reproduced.

While an experienced clinician may use this test successfully, it does not lend itself to "cook book" interpretation or use by inexperienced examiners, nor should it be used in making final determinations regarding organic brain dysfunction, perceptual-motor deficits, or personality malfunction.

A few highly skilled clinicians can piece together some good hunches about a subject from the drawings, but since they rely on hunches, the Bender-Gestalt remains an experimental instrument, and validation studies prove disappointing despite extensive use. Most social service practitioners would not find the Bender-Gestalt test results useful in decision making. How, for example, would a social worker use a test report indicating "suspicion of organicity"? The results of this test should be regarded with caution.

The Culture Fair Intelligence Test

A paper-and-pencil test developed by Cattell and Cattell and published by the Institute for Personality and Ability Testing, the *Culture Fair Intelligence Test* is available for three age levels, ranging from children to adults. The test's purpose is to provide a measure of ability directed at separating the evaluation of natural intelligence independent from cultural learning experiences. The Culture Fair Intelligence Test uses the classical I.Q., with a mean of 100 and a standard deviation of 16. The best available research on the test indicates that when used in industrial countries similar to the United States the results are consistent from country to country. In dissimilar countries, however, the results are significantly different from those obtained with the standardization sample. *Extreme caution is urged in interpreting the results of this test for persons who come from markedly different cultures.* The Institute for Personality and Ability Testing, in Champaign, Illinois, offers a manual providing more information about this test.

Tests for the Blind

Several standard tests, including the Stanford-Binet and Wechsler scales, have been adapted for use with blind persons. The *Interim Hayes-Binet Scale* is composed of items in the Stanford-Binet L and M, which do not require vision for completion. Currently, a special adaptation of the Wechsler scale is used widely for testing the blind. The major adaptation of the Wechsler omits the performance subtests.

Also available is the *Haptic Intelligence Scale for Adult Blind,* which was designed to test blind adults aged sixteen and above. Results are reported in the form of deviation I.Q.s, with a mean of 100 and a standard deviation of 15. The test manual, published by Psychology Research in Chicago and authored by Shurrager and Shurrager, contains further information. The test also is described in Buros' *Mental Measurements Yearbook.**

Tests for the Hearing Handicapped

Several tests have been used to assess the mental ability of people who are hearing handicapped: The *Nebraska Tests of Learning Aptitude,* the *Pintner-Peterson Performance Scale,* the *Arthur Point Scale,* and the *Point Scale of Performance.*

The Point Scale of Performance is available in two forms from C. H. Stoelting Company and the Psychological Corporation. Both are designed to test persons from five years of age to adulthood. The purpose of the scale is to provide a measurement of the intellectual ability of deaf children, children suffering from reading handicaps, and non-English-speaking children. The test was standardized on 1,100 public school

---

*O. K. Buros, ed., *Mental Measurements Yearbook,* 7th ed., 2 vols. (Highland Park, New Jersey, Gryphon Press, 1972).

children from middle-class American homes. Scores are reported in the form of mental-age norms and a ratio I.Q.

Tests for the Orthopedically Handicapped

The *Pictorial Test of Intelligence,* available through Houghton Mifflin Company, requires neither manipulative nor speaking responses. It was designed to assess the general intelligence ability of children between the ages of three and eight. It also can be used to test children who are orthopedically handicapped and cannot respond orally or in writing. The manual provides information with regard to deviation I.Q. norms, mental-age norms, and percentile norms. Scores may be reported in all three forms.

Other tests that have been used with the orthopedically handicapped include the *Progressive Matrices Test,* the Peabody Picture Vocabulary Test, and the *Columbia Mental Maturity Scale.*

CHAPTER 8

TEST REPORTS

IN Chapter 6, How to Make a Test Referral, a suggested guide for test referrals was presented. A copy of the test referral should be kept with the test report. In most cases, test reports and accompanying information are retained for possible future use. The test report also should contain information, in addition to test results and interpretations, that will make the information optimally useful on future occasions. Suggested supplementary information is outlined in the following section.

SUGGESTED GUIDE FOR SUPPLEMENTARY TEST REPORT INFORMATION

1. Description of examinee, including —
   a. name
   b. age at date of testing
   c. sex
2. Test information, including —

a. date of testing
b. place of testing
c. tests administered
3. Examiner information, including—
a. name and title
b. licenses
c. affiliation

If the supplementary test report information, test report, and test referral are retained, the test report will be easy to refer to and use in the future.

CONFIDENTIALITY

Psychological tests often are the point of discussion when the issue of confidentiality is raised. Before being tested, a client should be made aware of what to expect in the testing situation, how the test information will be used, and who will have access to the test results.

Test results frequently are overemphasized. Although test results may reveal measures of personality traits, intelligence, interests, and aptitudes, clients usually do not realize that the results only estimate characteristics. Actually, in many instances, persons close to the client observe a vast amount of behavior that would yield better estimates. Although most people attribute to psychological tests powerful properties that they do not possess, confidentiality always is of concern.

Safeguarding information about a client, including test reports, should be a primary obligation for anyone with access to the information. Violations of clients' rights to confidentiality can cause personal conflicts and damage the reputation of the social service practitioner and agency involved. A set of ethical standards* proposed by the American Psychological Association deals directly with the issue of confidentiality. Principle 6b states: "Information obtained in clinical or consulting relation-

---

*American Psychological Association, "Ethical Standards of Psychologists," *American Psychologist*, *18*:58-59, 1963.

ships, or evaluative data concerning children, students, employees, and others, are discussed only for professional purposes and only with persons clearly concerned with the case. Written and oral reports should present only data germane to the purposes of the evaluation; every effort should be made to avoid undue invasion of privacy." Confidentiality is an important concept that protects clients, social service practitioners, and agencies.

SAMPLE TEST REPORTS

Examples of the main body of test reports are provided in the following sections to introduce the psychological jargon and general writing style employed. Reports are listed in alphabetical order. It is important to remember that these reports are taken out of context and would not be used without the complete test report.

Bender-Gestalt: Test Report

There is evidence of some mild, diffuse organic damage that probably occurred in early childhood, perhaps between four and seven years of age and possibly owing to an encephalitic condition. Although she has partially compensated for the intracranial damage, the organic factor presents a handicap. At present, however, her central problem appears to be neurotic inhibition accompanied by some depression and apathy. The organic factor contributes to her adjustment difficulties but is insufficient to explain them. Her prime means of defense are withdrawal, denial, and isolation. She is fearful of rejection, especially at the hands of those she perceives as authority or parental figures. While she usually tries to conform on a conscious level, she shows fairly pronounced passive, oppositional tendencies. Under stress, there may be some regression to narcissism and orally dependent behavior. Despite this, she shows progression and has established some behavioral configurations characteristic of both anal and oedipal periods of adjustment. She needs closeness with people but is fearful of interpersonal relationships and has not developed skills for encouraging them. She remains in superficial, rather distant relationships, while embellishing them with fantasy. At present, she is moderately depressed, partly because she does not get the attention she needs and partly because of guilt over impulses that she ordinarily inhibits. At this point, she seems to be especially fearful of heterosexual relationships and may suffer from unresolved sexual feeling for her father. Although her major identification is female, her self-image is that of an inadequate person. Characteristically, she is withdrawn, aloof, and rather "retarded" in her behavior.

An estimate of her intellectual abilities measured by her present Bender performance would yield an I.Q. of approximately 75, a rough estimate that probably characterizes her present school performance but is not a good reflection of her potential. Despite her attempt to cooperate on the test, there is considerable evidence of marked impairment of intellectual functioning owing to neurotic problems. If her neurotic difficulties were resolved and her severe inhibitions were overcome, she probably would function within or near the average range of intelligence.

California Psychological Inventory: Test Report

The results suggest an individual who is sensitive to evaluation by others of his behavior. This may lead to strong attempts to impress significant others in social situations. For example, he likely will try to be the center of attention at social gatherings through story telling and extroverted acts. His outward behavior belies apparent inner feelings of inferiority and low self-esteem. In fact, the subject's extroversion may be an attempt to counter his feeling of inadequacy.

Perhaps a more positive compensatory mechanism is shown in the subject's strong motivation to accomplish and achieve. This may be the strongest force in determining his behavior and, coupled with logical thought processes relatively free from anxiety, suggests a successful economic future.

General Aptitude Test Battery: Test Report

The subject's scores on the Intelligence, Verbal Aptitude, and Numerical Aptitude sections of the General Aptitude Test Battery indicate that his achievement is far above average in each of these categories. His Intelligence score is at the 99th percentile compared with the general working population, while his Verbal and Numerical scores compared with the same population are at the 96th percentile. All his scores on the remaining aptitudes of the battery are at the 75th percentile or above, including his scores on the Manual and Finger Dexterity Form Board. It is apparent, then, that he is capable intellectually of undertaking technical or college training in any of the occupational aptitude patterns covered by the GATB; that is, he has the intellect and dexterity necessary to handle any of the many occupational categories listed from Occupational Aptitude Pattern 1 through 35. His interest profile from the other tests in the battery suggests that he may wish to consider any of the following occupations listed in Occupational Aptitude Pattern 1: physician, civil engineer, highway engineer, etc. Under Occupational Aptitude Pattern 2, he may wish to consider training as a pharmacist, cost accountant, tax accountant, or statistician. Appropriate occupations from Occupational Aptitude Pattern 3 include teacher, survey worker, group worker, or caseworker.

Strong-Campbell Interest Inventory: Test Report

Test results indicate a client highly interested in religious activities, social service, music, public speaking, business management, art, teaching, mathematics, and technical supervision. His general interests show a similarity to those of men successful as music teachers or performers, as well as credit managers, chamber of commerce executives, business education teachers, social workers, YMCA staff members, rehabilitation counselors, public administrators, physical therapists, and librarians. Surprisingly, in view of his stated vocational aspirations of computer programming, his interests do not parallel those of computer programmers. With this in mind, he should revise his career plans.

While computer science is not an inappropriate career choice, the client probably would be happier in a career oriented more toward administration and dealing with the public. Computer science might provide an opportunity for this, especially if supplemented with general business and/or management courses. He also may wish to consider a business curriculum, college, or trade school. Since counseling appeals to him, various types of social work may be feasible. Because of his ardent interest in music, however, he first should explore the possibilty of becoming a music teacher or performer.

Thematic Apperception Test: Test Report

The client's responses to the TAT indicate a chronically anxious, impulsive person who becomes flighty, disorganized, and hypermanic under stress. He avoids close relationships because he can relate only in a superficial, exploitive way. He wishes that those stronger than himself would take care of him, and he may go to great lengths to make people he sees as superior notice him. He has a negative, poorly defined identity. He feels alone, helpless, and unable to function without high anxiety unless involved in a constant frenzy of activity. His feminine interests do not equip him to compete with more aggressive peers. While he is not an overt homosexual, he may be primarily homoerotic in his sexual responses. He fears exploitation and attack.

Because the client is afraid of failure, he may not complete tasks. He has many personality deficits and functions in a way that will interfere with constructive achievement in a vocational training program. In fact, enrollment in a training program probably should be made contingent on regular psychological treatment. The subject will respond best to a supportive, problem-solving approach and behavior modification techniques emphasizing reward for constructive efforts.

Wechsler Adult Intelligence Scale: Test Report

The client is functioning within the normal range of intelligence. On the WAIS, she achieved a Verbal I.Q. of 92, a Performance I.Q. of 95, and a Full Scale I.Q. of 93. Her vocabulary is smaller than average. She thinks in a slightly "scattered" way and has trouble completing tasks requiring concentration or systematic organization of intellectual material. There is great variability in her intellectual performance, which is typical of the intellectual functioning of those who experience severe anxiety. In this client's case, the results are blocking, inattention to detail, mild confusion, and diminished ability to maintain cognitive set. She works better at structured and unambiguous problems than she does at those requiring her to be organized or to work out novel solutions. The degree of variability in her performance suggests that she would be functioning near the bright-normal range if she had been exposed to better learning opportunities and if she were not handicapped by chronic anxiety and emotional difficulties.

Wechsler Intelligence Scale
for Children: Test Report

The client is functioning in the bright-normal range of intelligence. On the WISC, he achieved a Verbal I.Q. of 112, a Performance I.Q. of 115, and a Full Scale I.Q. of 114. Although his relatively high scores on General Comprehension, Similarities, and Picture Arrangement indicate that he has considerable abstracting ability and his intellectual potential is quite high, the discrepantly low scores on Arithmetic, General Information, and Vocabulary reveal that he has been unable to make the most of his intellectual potential. Judging from his history and present living circumstances, the discrepancy probably is due to the effects of severe cultural deprivation. The relatively low score on Digit Span also suggests a significant level of anxiety that may be intrinsic to test situations. This often appears in children from culturally deprived environments and adds to the type of school underachievement that may be reflected in the subject's low scores on the Verbal subtests correlated with such achievement. Certainly, his high scores on Picture Completion, Block Design, and Object Assembly indicate superior perceptual-motor functioning and lend strength to the impression of substantially high intellectual functioning when measured by his overall performance on the Verbal subtests. His potential probably lies well within the superior range of intelligence (I.Q. = 120 to 130).

CHAPTER 9

HOW TO LEARN ABOUT
SPECIFIC TESTS

ALTHOUGH detailed information has been provided about a number of tests, the material presented is not intended to be a comprehensive reference guide describing all available tests. Following are some standard references that social service practitioners might use to obtain more information about specific tests.

The *Mental Measurements Yearbook*, edited by Oscar K. Buros, is revised periodically, so one should check for the latest edition. *Tests in Print*, by the same editor and publisher, is also revised at regular intervals.

Mental Measurements Yearbook lists most of the published standardized tests in print as of the year the edition was released. Those tests not reviewed in earlier editions are described and criticized by various authorities. *Tests in Print* is a comprehensive test bibliography and index providing the following information: name of test, levels for which it is intended, publication date, specialized comments about the test by authorities, number and types of scores provided, authors, publisher, and reference to test reviews in *Mental Measurement Yearbook*.

Other worthwhile reference books on testing are as follows:

Anastasi, A.: *Psychological Testing.* New York, Macmillan Publishing Co., 1976.

Berdie, R. et al.: *Testing in Guidance and Counseling.* New York, McGraw-Hill Book Co., 1963.

Cronbach, L. J.: *Essentials of Psychological Testing,* 3rd ed. New York, Harper and Row Pubs., 1970.

Robb, G., Bernardoni, L. C., and Johnson, R. W.: *Assessment of Individual Mental Ability.* New York, IED, 1972.

Thorndike, R. L. and Hagen, E.: *Measurement and Evaluation in Psychology and Education,* 3rd ed. New York, John Wiley & Sons, 1969.

Professional periodicals that regularly review recently published or revised tests include *Educational and Psychological Measurement, The Journal of Counseling Psychology, The Journal of Educational Measurement, and Personnel and Guidance Journal.*

The availability of detailed test information is an invaluable asset to persons engaged in the delivery of human services.

INDEX

Page numbers for table references are in italics.

This is a slender volume but it is packed with useful and usable information. It is presented for social workers, other human services practitioners and health professionals who lack specific training in the use of psychological tests and test reports. Interpretation and utilization of test information, rather than administration of such tests, are the primary topics of discussion.

The text presents information on the many types of available psychological tests, describes their uses and limitations, and offers detailed descriptions of some of the most commonly used tests. Sample test reports are included to demonstrate the format and content that may be expected. These sample reports also provide examples of the specialized, often esoteric vocabulary used by psychological examiners.

Psychological tests of every description are reviewed. Achievement and aptitude tests, intelligence tests, personality and interest tests, and special diagnostic tests are explained in detail. The authors also present information about the basic concepts of test design, construction, reliability, and validity. Statistical concepts — norms, measure of central tendency and variability, estimate of predictive error, and other statistical concepts — are thoroughly explained so that the reader may better understand and interpret the meanings of specific test scores.